Generative AI:

Content Creation, Personalization, and E-commerce at Scale for Marketers

By **GREG KIHLSTRÖM**

Published by:

Agile Brand, LLC

3100 Clarendon Boulevard #200

Arlington, VA 22201

https://www.gregkihlstrom.com

First Edition: November 2023

The publisher is not responsible for websites (or their content) that are not owned by the publisher.

Edited by Loretha Greene

Cover design and illustrations by Greg Kihlström

ISBN – 979-8-86-330514-1

To Lindsey,

my partner in agility.

Also by Greg Kihlström:

The Agile Series:

- *The Agile Brand* (2018)
- *The Agile Consumer* (2019)

Digital Delight First and Second Editions (2019 and 2020)

House of the Customer Series:

- *The Center of Experience* (2020 and 2023)
- *Meaningful Measurement of the Customer Experience* (2022)
- *House of the Customer* (2023)

Agile Brand Guides:

- *Conversational Marketing* (2023)
- *Creating an Agile Brand* (2023)
- *Customer Data Platforms (CDPs)* (2022)
- *Customer Journey Orchestration (CJO) Platforms* (2022)
- *Agile Marketing Fundamentals* (2023)
- *Agile Marketing Implementation* (2023)
- *Marketing & AI* (2023)
- *Marketing Measurement & Analytics (2023)*
- *Marketing Technology Platform Evaluation* (2023)
- *Marketing Operations* (2023)

Coming soon:

Priority is Action (2024)

Contents

Acknowledgments

As with any book, countless people had a hand in the thoughts and ideas contained within. I will endeavor to thank many of them, but a full list would take up its own book, so please excuse this abbreviated list.

I'm thrilled at the contributions from the marketing technology community to this book. I think it is a testament to the importance and timeliness of this topic. Thanks to Bernadette Nixon, CEO of leading enterprise search platform Algolia for contributing the foreword to this book. Thanks also to Tara DeZao of Pega, Kevin Li of Optimizely, and Infinum Managing Director Jonathan Boakes for their thoughts on generative AI that were incorporated into this book.

A special thanks to Juanita Solano for encouraging the swift release of this book, as my previous guide to AI & Marketing, while not even nearly six months old, still needed an update based on how quickly things are moving!

Thanks also to my wife Lindsey, who always supports me, no matter how many books I write during the course of a year (this year, it will have been a few!). She is forever an inspiration, and I'm thankful to have such a great partner in all things.

Finally, thank you to everyone reading this book, anyone who has listened to my podcast, read an article, and supported me in any way over the last several years. I hope that the thoughts and ideas shared by myself and others have been helpful in your work.

Let's move forward and create great things together!

Foreword

Generative AI represents the epitome of a technological marvel—a convergence of machine learning, neural networks, and creativity. Its fundamental principle is equivalent to a digital artist inspired by a vast repertoire of knowledge. Once trained on extensive datasets, Generative AI has the ability to create content autonomously by imitating patterns and styles from the data it has assimilated.

Greg Kihlström, best-selling author, podcaster, speaker, and entrepreneur, serves as an advisor and consultant to household brands on marketing technology, customer experience, and digital transformation initiatives. This focus positions him as a strategic visionary who can spot trends and guide people and businesses to new ways to innovate that marketers should pay attention to. His book, appropriately titled 'The Agile Brand Guide: Generative AI', serves as a guide for both the curious and the visionary – those looking to embrace the transformative (and disruptive) power of Generative AI in their marketing strategies.

Generative AI offers unparalleled possibilities to augment creativity, drive efficiency, and elevate brand agility. Indeed, according to McKinsey research, Generative AI is expected to add a staggering US$ 4.4 Trillion annually to the global economy.

The applications of Generative AI are as diverse as, and limited by, the extent of human imagination. From generating human-like text, designing visual art, and composing music to even producing realistic images, this Generative AI-driven creativity is making waves across industries. In the realm of content creation, Generative AI is poised to be a game-changer, addressing the challenges of producing vast amounts of diverse content with remarkable speed and quality.

To comprehend the profound impact of Generative AI on content creation, a deeper understanding of its functioning is essential. Greg Kihlström dips into how Generative AI operates on neural networks and is modeled after a human brain's structure and functioning. During the AI training phase, these neural networks learn intricate patterns, styles, and features from the datasets provided. Once trained, the AI can generate new content that mimics these learned patterns. This capability to create content at scale is a result of the AI's continuous learning, refining its abilities to craft compelling narratives, striking visuals, and more.

I liken the possibilities of Generative AI to how Algolia has built its AI Search offering for enterprise websites. Algolia has harnessed the combined power of large language models (LLMs) and retrieval-augmented generation (RAG) to understand the users' search intent, drive relevant, personalized results, and mitigate hallucinations at an unmatched level. For companies still tethered to antiquated search or other martech platforms, the time is now to step up to AI-powered knowledge discovery tools. Those that don't will find themselves providing subpar online experiences for their customers and will quickly face obsolescence.

A key area of focus for marketers is AI augmented content creation. The relationship between Generative AI and content creation is symbiotic. Generative AI augments and accelerates the content creation process, empowering creators to meet the growing hunger for diverse and engaging material. Greg Kihlström explores the nuances of this partnership and will show how Generative AI is not here to replace creators but to amplify and augment their capabilities, thus unleashing their untapped potential as well as enabling them to scale their efforts significantly.

Personally, I believe Generative AI's prowess in generating text is nothing short of remarkable. From drafting articles and blog posts to crafting product descriptions and advertisements, Generative AI can mimic various writing styles and tones. This means that a brand can harness this technology to consistently generate persuasive and informative content, enabling a more expansive digital presence.

Imagine a scenario where a marketing team tasked with creating a multitude of product descriptions can now leverage Generative AI to assist in generating compelling and unique descriptions for an extensive product line. This opens up possibilities for content creators to focus their energies on more creative and strategic tasks, while the AI handles the mundane and repetitive aspects of content generation.

Furthermore, by training the AI on diverse visual datasets, a brand can ensure that the generated visuals resonate with its style and branding. This has the potential to transform how designers and marketers approach their work, allowing for more rapid creativity and idea generation as well as the execution of visually appealing content for different segments of an audience.

The transformative and disruptive impact of Generative AI on content creation is far-reaching. It extends beyond simply addressing the challenges of scale, efficiency, and consistency. Greg Kihlström delves into the myriad benefits and the exciting possibilities that this technology holds for the world of content creation.

As we stand at the threshold of a new digital era, the future promises even more exciting advancements with Generative AI. Innovations in this field will elevate the quality and diversity of generated content, bringing us closer to a point where distinguishing between human and AI-generated content becomes a delightful challenge.

The possibilities are vast. We can envision a future where Generative AI truly improves a customer experience: imagine, for a moment, the idea of a digital device engaging with customers using human-like responses, where personalized advertising is driven by AI-generated creative campaigns, and where dynamic and interactive storytelling captivates audiences in ways we could only dream of... this dream, this future, is today! Are you ready?

Bernadette Nixon

CEO

Algolia

Introduction

At the risk of giving too much credit to a single source, it is hard to say if this book would exist without the introduction of ChatGPT, though there are many exciting and beneficial uses for generative AI that (as we will see) go well beyond that one application. While it is certainly not the only, or even arguably the *best,* of the generative AI platforms and tools, its launch in 2022 was undoubtedly the most successful online product launch ever achieved, with 100 million monthly active users within two months of launch[1].

Generative AI is the technology that has 42% of American workers making at least $100,000 per year saying that it will lead them to make more money in the next year[2]. Other statistics show fear of job replacement, and yet others show the promise of new potential careers and jobs being created. There is a lot of discussion, and time will tell before we can say definitively if some or all of the predictions are true. As in most cases, reality will be somewhere between both extremes, but I think a helpful quote comes from Barry Asin, President of Staffing Industry Analysts (SIA): "Generative AI won't take your job, but someone using it will.[3]"

That said, companies are not necessarily prepared for the wave of AI, and in particular generative AI technologies and use cases that they are being inundated with. Some recent research from Infinum shows that 78% of businesses are planning to invest in AI during the next 12 months, yet

26% are unsure how to integrate AI into their products in a meaningful way and 65% say they are unsure how to use their data effectively for digital transformation. Additionally 35% lack the right skills and expertise to implement and manage AI effectively[4]. What does all of this mean? Well, one thing in particular is that the enterprise knows they *need* to adopt AI, yet they are unprepared from a strategic, operational, and talent perspective to do so. I'm hoping this book, and the work of many others I know and collaborate with will help in this effort.

I have been fortunate to see many groundbreaking technologies and applications of those technologies introduced during my professional career. While some have caught on immediately, others have taken longer to gestate and come into widespread use. When it comes to AI, you could say that it is a decades-old overnight sensation, with its origins dating back to everything from Japanese professor Makoto Nishimura's robot Gakutensoku in 1929[5], Alan Turing's proposed machine intelligence test from 1950 (called The Imitation Game)[6], or Arthur Samuel, whose 1952 checkers program which was the first to learn the game independently[7], and who, in 1959 created the term "machine learning" in a speech about teaching machines to play chess better than humans[8]. Of course, there are countless examples of those working to bring about artificial intelligence in a more mature state. While there are many complex applications built around the concept of AI, early ones often relied on simple rules-based decisioning—think if this, then that—and did not have the ability to learn from past choices.

The rise of neural networks

In this book, we'll skip ahead to slightly more recent times. Beyond its basis in the broader discipline of artificial intelligence, generative AI relies more heavily on a new approach to AI that emerged in the 1990s: neural networks. These, too, had their origins around the 1950s with Donald Hebb writing *The Organization of Behavior*, which highlighted that neural pathways grow stronger each time they are used, which is core to how people learn[9]. Similarly, neural networks are designed to work and learn much like the human brain, and they can evolve and learn from the data they are provided in a way that exceeds the capabilities of a simpler rules-based AI approach.

After some false starts in the 1960s and 70s, neural networks began to get more attention in 1982 when Jon Hopfield presented a paper at the National Academy of Sciences, while Japan announced its intentions to restart its effort to build neural networks (at that time in their fifth generation)[10]. At this point, progress was much quicker, and skipping forward a few decades, we have the tools available today, along with cloud availability, easier access to data, and more that enable generative AI tools to be created easier than ever.

Because neural networks can learn and adapt, it means that they are more flexible as far as their inputs are concerned, and it also means that they can get better without direct human intervention.

Building on neural networks is another important advance that has made generative AI possible: deep learning, a type of machine learning that relies on neural networks to learn from data. It took many years and innovations, from Fei-Fei Li, an AI professor at Stanford, launching ImageNet, a free database of 14 million labeled images that neural networks could train on in 2009, to Google Brain's 2012 project known as The Cat Experiment, which used a neural network spread over 1,000 computers to identify pictures of cats[11]. Another big innovation is the Generative Adversarial Neural Network (GAN), introduced in 2014 by Ian Goodfellow, where two neural networks play against each other in a game and learn from one another, thus continually improving the results.

Because of deep learning, built on the foundation of neural networks, Generative AI has achieved levels of realism and creativity in the past few years. This can be attributed to the availability of data, advances in computing power, as well as new algorithms that researchers have been able to create specifically for generative AI.

Why Generative AI?

Building on foundational artificial intelligence, neural networks, and deep learning that came before it, generative AI is the technique of designing AI that mimics human imagination and creativity. Unlike other fields of AI's focus on predictions and automation, generative AI enables machines to produce creative content, including text, images, and videos that mimic and go beyond human imagination. Applying generative AI in marketing means businesses can produce unique and compelling content on a large scale. This technology can help create innovative product designs, brand identities, and marketing campaigns that capture the interest of their target audience.

Generative AI has also helped to improve audience engagement through personalized marketing campaigns. Personalization is a critical strategy in today's marketing world as it helps connect with customers more emotionally. With its application, businesses can create unique and personalized content that appeals to their target audience, resulting in a higher conversion rate. One great example is 'The Next Rembrandt,' a project created by ING Bank[12]. With the help of AI-powered generative algorithms, they created a new Rembrandt painting by analyzing his previous works and style. The painting went viral, with the media coverage attracting massive attention online, making it the ultimate example of personalized marketing.

Generative AI also has significant implications for e-commerce, specifically in product recommendations as well. By analyzing customer data, generative AI can provide personalized and relevant customer recommendations based on their previous purchases. This technology can help to increase sales, improve customer engagement and loyalty, and reduce cart abandonment rates. A practical example is Amazon's AI-powered product recommendation system, which recommends relevant products based on customers' previous search and purchase history.

Suffice it to say generative AI is an innovative technology with the potential to impact marketing in many ways, and this guide will endeavor to explore many of them. The ability to produce creative content, improve audience engagement, create personalized marketing materials, and provide relevant product recommendations will mean substantial competitive advantages for early adopters. Understanding the basic principles of generative AI is essential for businesses looking to stay ahead of the competition in the future.

This guide is based on research . . . and experience

My work continually informs my writing, and this book is an example of that. I have been privileged to work with enterprise organizations of varying sizes (from Fortune 50 to 1000) and assisted with strategy creation, solution finding, and delivering many types of initiatives with which the approaches to AI adoption and implementation described in this book can help teams achieve better marketing results. I am committed to being both a writer-researcher and a practitioner; I want my insights to be more than purely theoretical. I hope this makes the concepts on the page more actionable, insightful, and beneficial to you, the reader.

Who this book is for

This book is for marketing leaders and aspiring leaders who want to understand how to evaluate and implement generative AI tools within their marketing to increase their effectiveness and efficiency in creating work that performs well according to marketing and business KPIs, including CMO and marketing leadership, marketing management, and other marketing team members.

While we provide a short list of generative AI tools and platforms in the appendix, this guide is not meant to be a tutorial or a set of software reviews on individual platforms. There are many resources available that do a better job of that. Instead, This guide is meant to provide ideas and starting points for leaders and teams to consider adopting generative AI tools.

Also, this is a *guide,* not an *encyclopedia.* Therefore, it is intended to be a short read and to quickly and easily give you a good understanding, though to get more in-depth knowledge, more reading, training, and experience will be required.

What We Will Cover

I'm excited to share my knowledge of generative AI approaches and tools with you over the pages that follow. This Agile Brand Guide is divided into three main sections:

- **Part 1: Background & Strategic Considerations**
  This section will give an overview of generative AI from a foundational and business perspective. We'll talk about why it is important to take it so seriously and how to look at it from a strategic and business context.
- **Part 2: Marketing Applications of Generative AI**
  In this section, we will look at several ways that generative AI can be used within the marketing discipline. We may not cover *every* way, but we'll do our best!

- **Part 3: Generative AI in Practice**
  In the last section, we will explore what it means to incorporate generative AI in your marketing from a goal-setting, operations, and results standpoint.

I've tried to strike a balance between giving an overview of why it makes sense to adopt generative AI and discussing practical examples of utilizing generative AI in marketing effectively.

Additional Resources

You can find related resources, as mentioned within the chapters that follow, available on The Agile Brand Guide website at: https://agilebrandguide.com

This includes our listing of generative AI tools and platforms that are updated regularly. Although we include a sampling of that list at the end of this book, the latest list is always available on the website mentioned above.

Also, please contact me if you have any questions or would like to be pointed in the right direction. You can find me on LinkedIn or contact me through The Agile Brand Guide website.

Part 1:
Background & Strategic
Considerations

In this first section of our book on generative AI for marketers, we will explore the six areas in which generative AI excels. These areas include generation, extraction, summarization, rewriting, classification, and question answering.

We will then delve into why marketers need to understand generative AI and its potential impact on their industry. Finally, we will examine the business case for generative AI, including the benefits, challenges, and potential ROI for businesses that adopt this technology. By the end of this section, you will have a solid understanding of the opportunities and challenges presented by generative AI for marketers.

Let's get started!

1.0 What is generative AI and why is everyone talking about it so much?

Generative AI is a type of artificial intelligence capable of creating new and original content, such as images, music, and text. The origins of generative AI can be traced back to the early days of artificial intelligence research in the 1950s and 1960s.

One of the earliest examples of generative AI is the work of mathematician John Horton Conway, who developed the concept of "cellular automata" in the 1970s. Cellular automata is a type of algorithm that uses simple rules to generate complex patterns, and it was later used as the basis for generative AI techniques such as genetic algorithms and evolutionary strategies.

Another important milestone in the development of generative AI was the creation of the first artificial neural network in the 1940s by researchers at the Massachusetts Institute of Technology (MIT). This early neural network was capable of learning to recognize patterns in data, and it laid the foundation for later generative AI techniques that use neural networks to generate new content.

In the 1980s and 1990s, researchers at MIT and other institutions developed new generative AI techniques, such as genetic algorithms and evolutionary strategies, inspired by natural evolution principles. These techniques were used to generate new and original content, such as images and music, by using a process of trial and error to evolve complex patterns and structures.

In the 21st century, the development of generative AI has been driven by advances in computing power and the availability of large amounts of data. Generative AI techniques such as deep learning and generative adversarial networks (GANs) have been used to generate highly realistic and diverse content, including images, videos, and music. These techniques use complex mathematical models to generate new content based on patterns and structures learned from large datasets.

The development of generative AI has been driven by a series of important milestones and breakthroughs, from the creation of the first artificial neural network in the 1940s to the development of deep learning and generative adversarial networks in the 21st century. These techniques have enabled the creation of highly realistic and diverse content, and they have a wide range of applications in fields such as entertainment, advertising, and scientific research.

Of course, as I mentioned in the introduction, there is one big reason generative AI has become such a hot topic lately, with many fast followers. ChatGPT's success brought to light this technology and approach, which has been around for years yet suddenly caught the attention of the public and the average business user. Generative AI is an idea whose time has come.

Let's acknowledge the hype

Of course, there is some hype around this technology. Okay, *more* than *some.* But is the hype justified, or will we all be rolling our eyes at the mention of AI or tools like ChatGPT a few years from now?

We've also had more than a few technology buzzwords and areas full of hype that haven't fulfilled the potential of the billions of dollars of investment…at least just yet. I'm thinking of the metaverse as a place of commerce, or NFTs as a bankable investment, to name a few. I spoke with Jonathan Boakes, Managing Director of a digital agency that works with a number of technologies, including generative AI about the hype cycle and generative AI. Here's what he had to say:

> *"Generative AI has created immense hype which can be justified based on its transformative potential. However, we've witnessed similar hype cycles in recent years with technologies like NFTs, Web3 and cryptocurrencies where people are caught between the excitement of new possibilities and the anxiety of unknown risks and challenges.*
>
> *It's essential to approach hype with a degree of caution. While developers are excited about what Generative AI can do particularly as the value of generative AI becomes evident as users integrate it into their workflows, it should be seen as a tool that*

complements existing processes and workflows. As a sidekick to operations, not a leader.

It is worth noting that although there is hype today, machine learning teams have been working in this space for years, delving into aspects like data analysis, game theory, and model building. For them, Generative AI isn't part of a hype cycle, it reflects an evolution, rather than a complete revolution.

For the hype of Generative AI to last, it relies on how ethically and effectively it is built and used."

To paraphase, it's kind of up to all of us to help make the promise of generative AI a reality, and we should all proceed with deliberacy and caution. This is something we'll talk about quite a bit later in the book.

I also asked Tara DeZao, Product Marketing Director at Pega, a company doing many innovative things in this area, what she thought about the *level* of hype that generative AI is getting concerning the benefits it can provide, and here's what she said:

"I do think the hype is justified because it will fundamentally change the way that we function as professionals daily, irrespective of the industries we are in. From areas like code generation to content production, customer support, product design, application development, reporting, risk management, fraud detection – the list goes on. Formerly human labor, especially around repetitive tasks, can now be automated with generative AI.

We're already seeing its usage for these purposes in Financial Services, Life Sciences, Software Development, Travel, Creative Agencies etc. AI, as a whole, gives us the ability to scale a business that humans just can't do. That said, there are also risks as well as functions that humans will never be replaced. For example, there is a lot of hype around GenAI taking away creative roles. I do think that from a production standpoint, there are manual tasks like content versioning that GenAI can help with, but for the big ideas, the true creativity? Nothing can replace humans."

I tend to agree with Tara that the hype is at least mostly justified, but also that this latest generation of AI tools not only reinforces how valuable and beneficial artificial intelligence can be to humans and their businesses but also how valuable and beneficial *humans* are in the equation as well.

Here's why AI is different than other recent fads

As of the writing of this book, generative AI is in the "Peak of Inflated Expectations[13]" stage of Gartner's Hype Cycle[14], which is followed by the "Trough of Disillusionment," which means that after that, we're going to actually achieve greater gains as it moves into the "Slope of Enlightenment" (the next phase). Gartner notes that the speed with which generative AI is moving is notable, and I will say from my own experience that the hype around generative AI is different from other technology fads for several reasons, all of which we'll discuss in greater detail in the pages that follow in this book:

1. **Immediate Usefulness:** Unlike other technologies that require significant investment and time to implement, generative AI can immediately be useful to organizations of all sizes. It can be applied to various industries and use cases, making it a versatile technology that can be leveraged in various ways. Kevin Li, VP of Product Strategy at Optimizely put it this way:

    "What's different about Generative AI, especially the initial use cases, is that, unlike some recently-hyped technologies like the metaverse or NFTs, is that it's almost immediately solving a pain point. So I think that's also why we have just a different adoption curve. Because the problem statement is much more obvious."

2. **Benefits Across Roles:** Generative AI can benefit many different organizational roles, from interns to senior knowledge workers. This technology can assist with brainstorming and idea generation, content creation, and analysis of metrics and feedback. As a result, generative AI has the potential to be useful to a large portion of the workforce, making it a more inclusive technology than some other fads that may only benefit specific departments or roles.

3. **Cross-Industry Applicability:** Generative AI can be applied to various industries, including healthcare, finance, marketing,

and education. This broad applicability makes it a more promising technology than others that may only be suitable for a specific industry or use case.

4. **End-to-End Process Improvement:** Generative AI can assist with multiple stages of a process, from brainstorming to content creation to feedback analysis. This end-to-end process improvement makes generative AI a more comprehensive technology than others that may only focus on a single aspect of the process.

5. **Immediate Real-World Benefits:** Generative AI has numerous real-world use cases, such as creating personalized content for customers, generating product descriptions, or assisting with medical diagnosis and treatment. These practical applications make generative AI a more viable technology than some other fads that may be more theoretical in nature.

6. **Scalability:** Generative AI can be scaled up or down depending on the organization's needs, making it a flexible technology that can adapt to changing business requirements.

7. **Cost-Effectiveness:** Generative AI can be a cost-effective solution for organizations, as it can automate many tasks that would otherwise require significant time and resources to complete manually. This cost-effectiveness makes generative AI more accessible to organizations of all sizes.

8. **Rapid Development:** The development of generative AI has been rapid, with significant advancements in recent years. This

fast pace of innovation ensures that the technology remains relevant and continues to improve over time.

9. **Wide-Ranging Impact:** Generative AI has the potential to impact various aspects of business operations, from product development to marketing to customer service. Its wide-ranging impact makes it a more comprehensive technology than others that may only focus on a single aspect of the organization.

10. **Holistic Approach:** Generative AI takes a holistic approach to problem-solving, considering multiple factors and variables when generating solutions. This holistic approach ensures that the technology is well-rounded and can address complex challenges more effectively than other technologies that may focus on a single aspect of the problem.

Because of these reasons and more, generative AI stands out from other technology fads due to its immediate usefulness, benefits across roles, cross-industry applicability, end-to-end process improvement, real-world use cases, scalability, cost-effectiveness, rapid development, wide-ranging impact, and holistic approach.

Six areas where Generative AI excels

That said, as with any tool (or any shiny object that the marketing world fixates upon), there are good times to use it and not-so-good time. We should start, then, by looking at what generative AI does *well* so we can then explore how best to use it in marketing and customer experience work. To understand the true benefits of generative AI, it is important to look at the six main areas where it can be (and has proven to be) effective. Let's explore each of these now.

Areas where Generative AI excels

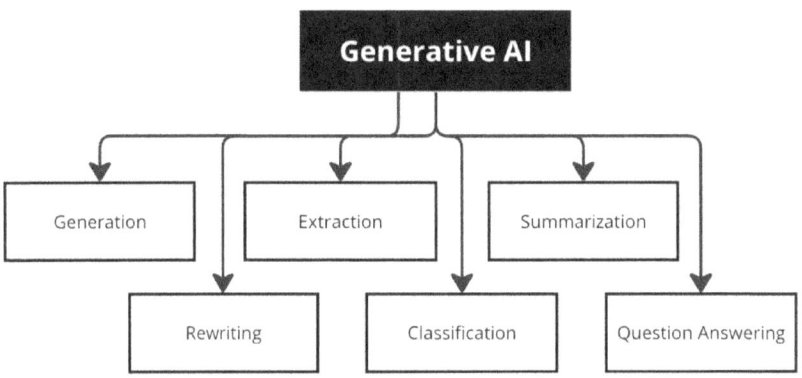

Figure 1.0.1, Six areas where Generative AI excels

Generation

One of the key applications of generative AI in content creation is in natural language generation (NLG). NLG is a subfield of AI that focuses on generating human-like text from structured data. This can be used to automatically generate articles, summaries, and other types of content based on a given input.

For example, a news organization could automatically use NLG to generate articles based on a set of pre-defined templates. The templates could include the basic structure of the article, such as the headline, introduction, and conclusion, as well as specific details, such as the names of the people involved and the event's location. The NLG system would then fill in the details based on the input data, such as the results of a sports game or the latest political developments.

Another application of generative AI in content creation is in text completion. Text completion is a language model trained to predict the next word or sentence in a given text. This can be used to automatically complete sentences or paragraphs that are left incomplete, such as in a blog post or social media update.

For example, a social media platform could use text completion to automatically complete sentences or paragraphs that users leave incomplete in their posts. The platform could use a language model to predict the most likely completion based on the user's previous posts and the platform's overall content.

In addition to natural language generation and text completion, generative AI can also be used in other areas of content creation, such as image and video generation. For example, a retail company could use generative AI to automatically generate images of products in different settings or with different backgrounds. This could be used to create more engaging product listings on the company's website or social media channels.

Generative AI is a powerful tool for content creation that can be used in various ways. By automating the content creation process, generative AI can help organizations save time and resources while increasing the quality and quantity of their content. Additionally, generative AI can help organizations personalize and customize their content better to meet the needs and preferences of their audience.

Extraction

Generative AI can be used to extract specific information from large amounts of text and data using techniques such as text classification and text clustering. These techniques allow the AI model to analyze large amounts of text data and identify patterns and trends that are relevant to a particular topic or subject.

For example, a generative AI model could be trained on a set of customer reviews for a particular product. The model could then be used to classify the reviews based on their sentiment, such as positive, negative, or neutral. The resulting information could be used to identify common issues or concerns customers have with the product or areas where the product excels.

Overall, generative AI can be a powerful tool for extracting specific information from large amounts of text and data. Using advanced techniques such as text classification and text clustering, generative AI can help organizations gain valuable insights from their data and make more informed decisions.

Summarization

Generative AI tools can be used to summarize information out of vast amounts of text, data, and other sources of information in a number of ways. One of the most common applications of generative AI in summarization is the use of natural language processing (NLP) algorithms. These algorithms can analyze large amounts of text and identify the most important information, such as key phrases, topics, and entities.

For example, a news organization could use generative AI to summarize articles for their website or social media channels automatically. The AI system would analyze the articles and identify the most important information, such as the main topic, key phrases, and important quotes. This information could then be used to create a short summary of the article that is easy for readers to understand.

Another way that generative AI can be used for summarization is through the use of machine learning algorithms. These algorithms can be trained on large amounts of data and learn to identify the most important information in a text. For example, a financial organization could use generative AI to summarize reports and other financial documents. The AI system would be trained on a large dataset of financial reports and would learn to identify the most important information, such as key trends and insights.

In addition to NLP and machine learning algorithms, generative AI can also be used for summarization through rule-based approaches. These approaches use a set of predefined rules to identify the most important information in a given text. For example, a legal organization could use generative AI to summarize contracts and other legal documents. The AI system would use a set of predefined rules to identify key terms and conditions in the contracts, making it easier for lawyers and other professionals to understand the contents of the documents quickly.

Generative AI is a powerful tool for summarization in various industries and applications. Using NLP, machine learning, and rule-based approaches, generative AI can help organizations quickly and accurately summarize large amounts of text, making it easier for readers and professionals to understand complex information.

Rewriting

Generative AI can rewrite existing content using techniques such as text summarization, text synthesis, and text generation. These techniques allow the AI model to analyze existing content and generate new content similar in style and structure, but this may contain new information or insights.

For example, a generative AI model could be trained on a set of news articles about a particular topic. The model could then be used to summarize the key points from the articles or synthesize new content by combining information from multiple articles. The resulting content would be similar to the original articles but may contain new insights or perspectives not present in the original content.

Overall, generative AI can be a powerful tool for rewriting existing content, similar to how it can generate original content from a prompt. Using advanced techniques such as text summarization, text synthesis, and text generation, generative AI can help automate the process of creating new content and make it easier for businesses to keep their content up-to-date and relevant.

Classification

Classification is one of the aspects of generative artificial intelligence that involves using algorithms to assign a label or category to a given piece of text or data. This process is also known as text classification or text categorization. The goal of classification is to automatically identify the topic or category of a given text based on its content.

There are several different approaches to text classification, including rule-based methods, statistical methods, and machine-learning algorithms. Rule-based methods involve defining a set of rules or patterns used to classify text. For example, a rule-based approach to classification might involve identifying the presence of certain keywords or phrases associated with a particular category.

Statistical methods, on the other hand, rely on statistical models to predict the category of a given piece of text. These models are typically trained on a labeled dataset, where the text is annotated with its corresponding category. The model is then used to make predictions on new, unlabeled text.

Machine learning algorithms are a more advanced approach to text classification. These algorithms use complex mathematical models to learn patterns in the data and make predictions about new text. Several different types of machine learning algorithms can be used for text classification, including decision trees, support vector machines, and neural networks.

One of the key applications of text classification is in natural language processing (NLP) tasks such as sentiment analysis, spam filtering, and topic classification. Sentiment analysis involves identifying the sentiment or emotion expressed in a piece of text, such as whether it is positive, negative, or neutral. Spam filtering involves identifying and filtering out unwanted or irrelevant email messages. Topic classification involves identifying the topic or category of a piece of text, such as whether it is about sports, politics, or technology.

Text classification can also be used in other applications, such as information retrieval, where it is used to categorize and index documents for search engines. It can also be used in text summarization, where it is used to identify the most important sentences or phrases in a document and extract them for summary.

Question answering

Generative AI-powered chatbots and virtual assistants utilize this technology to interact with customers naturally. They can understand the intent behind customer inquiries, generate appropriate responses, and offer personalized interactions. These chatbots are not limited to predetermined responses but can understand and adapt to customer queries and provide a range of responses, engaging customers in meaningful conversations.

Conclusion

Generative AI has proven a powerful tool in various areas, including generation, extraction, summarization, rewriting, classification, and question answering. These capabilities can potentially revolutionize industries such as journalism, marketing, and customer service. As technology advances, it will be interesting to see how it can be leveraged to improve our lives and solve real-world problems.

1.1 Why marketers need to understand Generative AI

Now that we've explored some of the history and background of generative AI, let's look at why it is particularly relevant to marketers. Marketing leaders and their teams are constantly looking for new ways to create engaging content and drive conversions, and one of the more exciting realms pushing innovations is generative AI. This powerful tool can generate high-quality content at scale, personalize campaigns for individual customers, and even create new product lines. However, to truly harness the power of generative AI, marketers need to understand some of the strategic implications as well as their effects on marketing operations.

In this chapter, we'll explore why generative AI is a game-changer for marketers and why it's essential to understand its capabilities and limitations. So, let's get started!

How Generative AI Changes Your Strategic Marketing Approach

Using generative AI well can include changes in the strategic approach and how work is prioritized and planned. Let's discuss a few of these, from generating personalized product recommendations to creating captivating social media content.

Changes to Strategic Approach:

1. **Personalization:** Generative AI enables marketers to create highly personalized content for individual customers, increasing engagement and conversions. By analyzing customer data, generative AI can generate product recommendations, email subject lines, and social media posts tailored to each customer's preferences and interests.

2. **Scalability:** Generative AI can produce high-quality content at scale, allowing marketers to create more content in less time. This enables teams to focus on higher-level creative tasks rather than spending hours crafting individual pieces of content.

3. **Innovation:** Generative AI can inspire new and novel marketing campaign ideas, helping teams break out of their comfort zones and explore fresh perspectives. By generating a list of potential product names or taglines, for example, generative AI can help marketers identify untapped opportunities and develop innovative campaigns that stand out in a crowded marketplace.

Changes to Prioritization and Planning

1. **Content Creation:** With generative AI, content creation becomes more strategic and efficient. Marketing teams can focus on developing high-level creative concepts while the generative AI platform handles the heavy lifting of content generation. This enables teams to prioritize their time and resources on the most impactful tasks.

2. **Data Analysis:** Generative AI can analyze large amounts of customer data to identify patterns and trends that can inform marketing strategy. By analyzing this data, marketers can gain insights into customer preferences and tailor their campaigns accordingly.

3. **Collaboration:** Generative AI can facilitate collaboration between team members by providing a shared platform for content creation and review. This enables teams to work together more effectively and streamline the content development process.

How Generative AI Changes Your Marketing Team Staffing Approach

In addition to evolving the fundamental areas of marketing *strategy,* one of the most important areas that AI has positively impacted is hiring and team planning. Thanks to generative AI tools, teams can work more efficiently, with greater speed and accuracy, and with less human error.

Now, let's explore the significant impact of generative AI on modern marketing teams, including writers, designers, and other team members who use these tools, and why it is crucial for marketing leaders to embrace this technology.

Automating Repetitive Tasks

Generative AI technology has revolutionized the marketing industry by allowing teams to automate repetitive tasks like copywriting, designing, and even video editing. With the push of a button, leading AI tools can generate quality content in seconds, freeing up valuable time for marketers to work on other important tasks.

Product companies like Grammarly, Canva, and Adobe Sensei have released ground-breaking tools that have not only improved the efficiency of modern marketing teams but also provided them with enhanced accuracy, creativity, and scientific insights.

Improved Collaboration

Another significant benefit of generative AI tools is the improved collaboration between team members. As teams become more globally distributed, AI tools have become a crucial communication bridge between different regions. These tools can also help to break down language barriers by providing real-time translation for team members who don't speak the same language. This saves time and money and promotes teamwork, better decision-making, and inclusivity.

Enhanced Creativity

Thanks to AI technology, marketers can now explore new possibilities and generate creative solutions that may have been impossible before. With AI tools, marketing teams can build mockups of websites, play with user interfaces, and experiment with new formats. The possibilities are endless, thanks to AI-driven algorithms that analyze past successes and create custom solutions to meet the target audience's needs. By leveraging these tools, marketers can stay ahead of the curve and develop groundbreaking ideas that establish them as industry leaders.

Improved Customer Experience

Finally, generative AI technology has significantly impacted customer experience and engagement. With AI tools, teams can now analyze customer feedback, social media activity, and industry trends, allowing them to make data-driven decisions and enhance overall customer satisfaction. By integrating AI-driven chatbots, websites, and personalization engines into their marketing strategies, organizations can improve the accuracy and efficiency of their customer engagement.

It is Changing the Creative Process

The creative process is an essential part of marketing, continually evolving with new technology. One of the biggest changes in recent years is the integration of generative AI into the creative process. AI is transforming marketing and has changed how marketing teams, writers, and designers approach their work.

Today, AI tools can assist with copywriting, graphic design, and even video creation. Let's explore how generative AI is changing the creative process for marketing teams and its impact on creative output and outcomes.

Kickstarting Initial Ideas

Generative AI can be a powerful tool to help kickstart creative ideas and the creative process for marketing teams. Generative AI can help marketers break out of their comfort zones and explore fresh perspectives by generating new and novel ideas, headlines, and even images.

For example, a generative AI platform could be used to generate a list of potential product names or taglines, helping to spark creativity and inspire new ideas. Additionally, generative AI can be used to create optimized images for specific social media platforms, helping increase engagement and drive conversions. By leveraging the power of generative AI, marketers can unlock their full creative potential and develop innovative campaigns that stand out in a crowded marketplace.

Moreover, generative AI can also help marketers overcome writer's block or lack of inspiration. By providing a constant stream of new ideas and suggestions, generative AI can help to keep the creative juices flowing and prevent marketers from getting stuck in a rut. For instance, a generative AI platform could generate a list of potential blog post topics or social media post ideas, helping keep content fresh and engaging. By leveraging these capabilities, marketers can stay ahead of the curve and continuously push the boundaries of what is possible in their campaigns. Overall, generative AI can revolutionize the creative process for marketing teams, unlocking new levels of innovation and success.

Increased Efficiency in Creative Work

One of the significant benefits of AI in marketing is that it can save a lot of time for marketing teams. With AI tools, writers can produce clear, concise, and engaging content in a matter of minutes.

For example, AI-powered writing tools like GPT-3 can generate a full article based on a simple prompt. Similarly, designers can use AI platforms like Canva to generate whole graphics for social media posts, presentations, and even website designs. These types of tools allow marketing teams to focus their time and energy on other essential tasks while AI does the heavy lifting.

Improved Accuracy in Creative Work

Aside from saving time, generative AI tools can remarkably improve the accuracy and quality of creative work.

For instance, AI algorithms can use data analysis to understand and recognize which type of content performs well on different platforms, creating more effective content. This can work well with SEO strategies, in which AI has the ability to generate highly optimized keyword-based content that ranks well in search engines. As a result, the creative output will be more targeted, relevant, and optimized for the target audience.

Customizable Creative Templates

Another advantage of AI is that it can create customizable templates that enable users to generate unique and original content without starting from scratch.

Templates can come pre-made with initial design and content elements, making it easier to focus on fine-tuning the content to fit the brand and message. AI tools can also adjust these templates based on audience analysis, making it simpler to focus on specific audience types. With customizable templates, marketers can efficiently produce a wide range of content, from email marketing campaigns to social media posts, without losing consistency or quality.

Innovation in Creative Ideas

One of the biggest benefits of generative AI in marketing is its ability to develop creative ideas. AI tools can come up with ideas that traditional creativity methods may not produce, and these ideas can open up new opportunities for brands in terms of innovative thinking and creative solutions.

Also, AI uses machine learning algorithms that enable it to discover patterns and create content formats that may have previously not been considered. Thus, marketers using AI can gain new perspectives and take new directions in their marketing strategies, catching their audiences' attention with new and innovative approaches.

Cost-Effective Creativity

Marketing budgets are still as critical as ever, which means spending on creative projects needs to be adequate and manageable. Generative AI in marketing can offer affordable, less expensive solutions than traditional models. There can be less need to outsource to expensive creative agencies or employ in-house designers, as AI tools can produce quality and effective creative products, even with limited budgets. This can help restore brands with less investment while still maintaining quality and innovation.

Marketing teams that embrace AI can realize better creative output, save time and money, and bring more value to their projects. Nonetheless, marketing leaders should approach these technologies carefully and ensure they are used in a strategic, targeted way. When leveraged properly, generative AI can be a powerful ally in the marketing landscape.

It is changing internal expectations

The advent of generative AI tools has revolutionized the way organizations approach marketing, design, and writing work. These tools enable teams to create highly realistic and diverse content more quickly and accurately, which has changed internal expectations around speed to market and the amount of effort and team members required to produce marketing, design, and writing work.

Time and cost to first (and final) draft

In the past, creating marketing, design, and writing work required a significant amount of time, effort, and resources. Teams had to manually design and create each piece of content, which was time-consuming and often resulted in inconsistencies and errors. However, with the advent of generative AI tools, teams can now create highly realistic and diverse content more quickly and accurately.

Democratizing creative capabilities

For example, generative AI tools can be used to create highly realistic images and videos, which can be used in marketing campaigns. These tools use complex mathematical models to generate new content based on patterns and structures learned from large datasets. This enables teams to create highly realistic and diverse content without manual design and creation, which saves time and resources.

More diverse content

In addition to saving time and resources, generative AI tools enable teams to create more diverse and creative content. These tools can generate content beyond the capabilities of human designers and creators, resulting in more unique and eye-catching content. This can be especially useful in industries where creativity is a key differentiator, such as fashion or entertainment.

However, while generative AI tools have many benefits, they also present some challenges. For example, there is a risk of over-reliance on these tools, which can lead to a lack of understanding of how they work and how to use them effectively. This can result in low-quality or inappropriate content being produced, damaging a brand's reputation.

To address these challenges, teams need to clearly understand how generative AI tools work and how to use them effectively. This includes understanding the limitations and potential biases of these tools and how to integrate them with other design and creation tools. By doing so, teams can leverage generative AI tools to create high-quality and diverse content more quickly and accurately while maintaining creative control and quality standards.

It is changing external expectations

In recent years, the marketing world has seen a major shift towards using generative AI tools in creating hyper-personalized content and images. This has revolutionized how businesses approach customer experiences and has presented unique opportunities to establish better customer relationships.

However, this shift has led to a change in customer expectations, with customers expecting the same level of personalization and speed from every company they encounter. In this blog post, we'll explore the evolution of customer expectations in the age of generative AI.

Increased Demand for Personalization

Customers have always appreciated personalized experiences, but the rise of generative AI has taken this to new heights. With the use of machine learning algorithms, companies can now create highly customized content in real time, making the customer feel seen and valued. This has led to increased customer expectations for personalization across all aspects of their interactions with companies, including product recommendations and customer service interactions.

Increased Expectations for Speed

Generative AI tools allow businesses to create content at a once-impossible speed. This has raised the bar for customer service response times, as customers now expect instant response times when they contact a company. AI-powered chatbots and automated responses have become essential to meet these high expectations and maintain positive customer relationships.

Heightened Need for Transparency

While AI-based personalization has the potential to create exceptional customer experiences, it also raises concerns about privacy and data usage. Customers now expect complete transparency surrounding how their data is being used and expect businesses to respect their privacy. Additionally, customers expect companies to be transparent about using AI in their operations, as it's become an increasingly common practice in the marketing world.

Increased Demands for Omnichannel Experiences

Generative AI tools have made it easier to create experiences tailored to individual customers on each channel they use. As a result, customers now expect companies to provide seamless experiences across all channels they utilize. Customers expect consistency in messaging and personalization, regardless of where they are in their customer journey.

The Desire for Human Connection

Despite the benefits generative AI tools bring to customer experiences, consumers still value human connection. While chatbots can help with simple inquiries, many customers prefer speaking to a human for more complex issues. This is particularly true in industries such as healthcare and finance, where the consequences of a miscommunication can be significant. As a result, businesses must strike a balance between the use of AI tools and providing human interaction.

Conclusion

There are a lot of ways, you could say, that generative AI is impacting organizations. Both in all of the individual ways I mentioned earlier, as well as holistically across all of these areas. I asked Tara DeZao from Pega where she thought marketers should pay specific attention to in the area of generative AI, and here's what she said:

> *"For marketers specifically, it's the ability to validate the impact of your content in real-time to see if it's resonating with audiences. Then, the ability to pivot and either generate new content on the fly or vary copy and tone and push creative in-flight almost instantly. This is a massive optimization of the campaign*

process. These are areas of campaign management and content creation that, in the past, have been highly dependent on human labor, processes, and approvals. Depending on the maturity of an organization, each channel could be operated in silos and often paid channels operated by external agencies. This means that campaign results would need to be gathered and aggregated by the operations team after a campaign has finished. You are looking at potential weeks to know if your creative and messaging are making an impact. Or if there was an issue with the creative, an error, or a negative placement. You'd have to pull that down and update the creative manually, then push it through approvals to push the creative back in flight—essentially wasting time and budget. With GenAI, marketers can now automate parts of the process that were just draining resources and burning employees out.

Another area GenAI is optimizing for marketers is audience simulation and persona validation, figuring out which audiences are likely to respond and which individual targets would have higher value or drive better performance before they are in production. GenAI is capable of auto-generating suggestions based on data analysis and testing. So the question "Is this the right audience?" can be answered ahead of time."

Generative AI is a powerful tool marketers must understand to stay ahead of the competition. By leveraging this technology, marketers can create personalized content at scale, unlock new levels of creativity and innovation, and meet the ever-changing needs of their target audience. As the digital landscape continues to evolve, generative AI will play an increasingly important role in shaping the future of marketing.

1.2 The Business Case for Generative AI

McKinsey estimates that generative AI could add the equivalent of roughly $3 trillion to the global economy, with 75% of that falling into customer operations, marketing and sales, software engineering, and R&D[15]. Similarly, a recent Gartner poll of 2,500 executives shows that 38% indicated that their investments in generative AI were centered around customer experience and retention. This was the primary focus, as indicated in the research, with the second highest priority being revenue growth, with 26% of respondents[16].

As a marketing leader, you know that staying ahead of the competition requires constant innovation and optimization. In the realm of marketing, generative AI tools offer a powerful solution for enhancing creativity, streamlining processes, and driving better results. Let's talk about some of the strategic reasons the organizations should be considering greater AI adoption, particularly where it can help in the realm of marketing and customer experience.

Getting great results at scale

Marketers are under pressure to deliver more tailored, personalized experiences to meet consumers' rising expectations. With the advent of generative AI, marketers can now leverage this technology to automate the work activities that absorb as much as 70% of employees' work time, allowing them to be more strategic and creative in their approach. Let's explore how generative AI transforms marketing work and enables marketers to deliver more efficiency and scale in their efforts.

Automating Repetitive Tasks

One of the primary benefits of generative AI is its ability to automate repetitive tasks that consume a significant amount of time and resources. Using machine learning algorithms to analyze data patterns, generative AI can generate reports, create content, and perform other tasks that are typically manual and time-consuming. This allows marketers to focus on higher-level strategic thinking and creativity rather than being bogged down by mundane tasks.

Enhancing Personalization and Customization

Generative AI also enables marketers to deliver more personalized and customized experiences for their audiences. By analyzing customer data and preferences, generative AI can create unique and relevant content that resonates with each consumer. This can include product recommendations, email marketing campaigns, and social media ads tailored to each customer's specific interests and needs.

Scaling Efficiency and Reach

One of the most compelling business cases for using generative AI is the time-saving capabilities it provides and generative AI's ability to understand natural language, which McKinsey notes comprises 25% of total work time, greatly accelerates brands' ability to respond and adapt to their customers through automation and greater efficiencies[17].

For instance, if an apparel retailer that sells several product lines on their multi-channel marketing platforms to multiple audiences in more than one region around the world needs to create a campaign, they need to create the following:

- Multiple variants of copy and materials for the **product** (e.g., shoes, shirts, jackets, etc.) and each **audience** (e.g., gender, age, HHI, etc.), with a different variation for each product/audience combination.
- Resizing and reformatting the materials for each **product** and **audience** combination for each **marketing channel** (e.g., social media platforms, email, website, mobile app)
- Unique **country/language combinations** (e.g., US English, UK English, Spanish, German, etc.) of materials for each audience on each marketing channel

Keep in mind that this doesn't account for personalized content that is tailored to the individual. This type of hyper-personalization can build on the above and tailor content to the individual based on things like:

- Recent purchase behavior and frequency of purchases (product purchases or return visits)
- Specific demographic information
- Customer loyalty information

As you can see, all of this adds up to a lot of variance and quite a bit of content to be created. Rest assured, though, generative AI is up to the task of scaling content creation to meet customer expectations for personalized content and experiences. Whether it is automation of text content variations or more advanced personalization, having the right team to set up a personalization strategy can take a generic-feeling marketing campaign and make it compelling and increase conversions.

With the capacity to analyze vast amounts of data and generate content at unprecedented speed, generative AI allows marketers to reach a larger audience and deliver more targeted campaigns with greater ease. This can include creating personalized emails and social media posts tailored to specific customer segments and generating product descriptions and other marketing materials in multiple languages.

Meeting Rising Consumer Expectations

As you well know, consumers expect more personalized and tailored experiences from the brands they interact with. Generative AI enables marketers to meet these rising expectations by delivering more customized content and offers that resonate with each consumer. By leveraging machine learning algorithms to analyze customer data and preferences, generative AI can help marketers create more effective marketing campaigns that drive engagement, conversions, and loyalty.

The Future of Marketing Work

As generative AI continues to evolve and mature, this technology will play a critical role in the future of marketing work. By automating repetitive tasks, enhancing personalization and customization, scaling efficiency and reach, and meeting rising consumer expectations, generative AI is set to revolutionize the way marketers approach their work. As the industry shifts towards more tailored, personalized experiences, generative AI will be at the forefront of this transformation, empowering marketers to deliver more effective and efficient campaigns that drive business results.

Generative AI is poised to revolutionize marketing work by automating repetitive tasks, enhancing personalization and customization, scaling efficiency and reach, and meeting rising consumer expectations. Generative AI will be at the forefront of this transformation, empowering marketers to deliver more effective and efficient campaigns that drive business results. With its ability to automate work activities, enhance personalization, scale efficiency and reach, and meet rising consumer expectations, generative AI is set to transform the future of marketing work in exciting and innovative ways.

Accelerating gains to the business from deeper customer insights

I'm sure I'm "preaching to the choir" by saying this, but marketers are under continually increasing pressure to deliver more tailored, personalized experiences to meet consumers' rising expectations. One of the key challenges in achieving this goal is understanding natural language, which comprises 25% of total work time, according to McKinsey.

However, generative AI is set to revolutionize marketing work by greatly accelerating brands' ability to respond and adapt to their customers through automation and greater efficiencies. In this article, we will explore three key points about how generative AI's ability to understand natural language can transform marketing work: improving speed to market and speed to outcomes, providing better reporting access to "citizen data scientists," and creating feedback loops that help both humans and AI learn and improve more rapidly.

Improving Speed to Market and Speed to Outcomes

Generative AI's ability to quickly parse large amounts of unstructured data provides up-to-the-minute insights, enabling marketers to respond to customer needs in real time. By automating the process of understanding natural language, generative AI can analyze vast amounts of customer feedback, social media posts, and other forms of unstructured data to provide real-time insights into consumer preferences and behavior. This allows marketers to quickly adapt their strategies and campaigns to meet changing customer needs, improving speed to market and speed to outcomes.

Providing Better Reporting Access to Citizen Data Scientists

Generative AI can more quickly understand what works and what doesn't, providing better reporting access to "citizen data scientists." By automating the process of understanding natural language, generative AI can provide more accurate and timely reporting on marketing campaigns and customer behavior. This allows marketers without extensive technical backgrounds to better understand their customers and make more informed decisions about their marketing strategies.

Creating Feedback Loops that Help Both Humans and AI Learn and Improve More Rapidly

Generative AI can help provide feedback loops that help both humans and AI learn and improve more rapidly by lowering technical barriers to interacting with and learning from data. By automating the process of understanding natural language, generative AI can create feedback loops that allow both humans and AI to learn and improve more rapidly. This allows marketers to quickly identify areas for improvement and adjust their strategies accordingly while also enabling AI to learn and improve over time through machine learning algorithms.

Generative AI's ability to understand natural language is a game-changer for marketing work. By improving speed to market and speed to outcomes, providing better reporting access to "citizen data scientists," and creating feedback loops that help humans and AI learn and improve more rapidly, generative AI is set to revolutionize how marketers approach their work. As the industry shifts towards more tailored, personalized experiences, generative AI will be at the forefront of this transformation, empowering marketers to deliver more effective and efficient campaigns that drive business results.

Optimizing the experience for customers and employees

As marketers, we strive to create more engaging and personalized experiences for our customers. With the advent of generative AI, we can now take our marketing efforts to the next level. By leveraging predictive analytics and generative AI together, we can create next best action content, offers, and experiences for our customers that drive greater engagement and conversions. In this article, we will explore three key points about how generative AI can revolutionize the way we approach marketing work: improving the employee experience, creating next best action content and experiences, and providing easier access to information and insights.

Improving the Employee Experience

With the ability to automate the work activities that absorb as much as 70% of employees' work time[18], generative AI provides an opportunity to allow humans to be more strategic and for the marketing work they perform to be more efficient and scale to meet consumers' rising expectations for more tailored, personalized experiences.

By automating tasks such as data entry, content creation, and customer service, employees can spend more time on strategic, substantive work that drives greater engagement and purpose. This, in turn, leads to increased employee satisfaction, lower turnover rates, and a more productive workforce.

Creating Next Best Action, Content, and Experiences

Predictive analytics and generative AI used together can create next best action content, offers, and experiences for customers. By analyzing customer data and behavior, marketers can use predictive analytics to identify patterns and trends that indicate what a customer is likely to do next. Generative AI can then be used to create personalized content and experiences tailored to the customer's needs and preferences. This leads to increased engagement, conversions, and customer loyalty.

Providing Easier Access to Information and Insights

Generative AI can improve the employee experience and the customer experience by providing team members with easier (low-code, no-code) access to information and insights that rely on generative AI's natural language abilities. By automating the process of understanding natural language, generative AI can provide faster and more accurate access to information and insights that help employees quickly answer customer questions and better understand the customers they are trying to reach. This leads to improved customer satisfaction, increased customer loyalty, and, ultimately, greater business success.

Generative AI is a powerful tool that can revolutionize how we approach marketing work. By improving the employee experience, creating next best action content and experiences, and providing easier access to information and insights, generative AI can help us deliver more engaging, personalized, and effective marketing campaigns that drive greater business success. As marketers, we must embrace this technology and leverage it to its fullest potential to stay ahead of the competition and meet the evolving needs of our customers.

Case study: Mercedes-Benz

As an example of how AI can be used in the enterprise, let's explore Mercedes-Benz from a recent podcast from McKinsey's Center for Future Mobility[19]. In it, Markus Schäfer, the head of Daimler AG's Mercedes-Benz Cars unit, discusses how the company is leveraging the power of chatbots and artificial intelligence (AI) to improve its customer service and product development. Here are a few highlights:

1. **AI in high gear:** Schäfer highlights that Mercedes-Benz is using AI in various areas, including production, logistics, and

customer service. The company has been experimenting with chatbots to improve its customer interactions.

2. **ChatGPT integration:** Schäfer mentions that Mercedes-Benz is working with a chatbot called ChatGPT, powered by the generative AI model GPT-3. This technology allows customers to communicate with the chatbot in natural language, and it can understand and respond to complex queries.

3. **Personalized customer service:** The chatbot enables Mercedes-Benz to provide personalized customer service, addressing specific issues and concerns of individual customers. Schäfer notes that this approach has led to higher customer satisfaction and better retention rates.

4. **Real-time data analysis:** AI is also being used to analyze real-time data from various sources, such as sensors in the vehicles and customer feedback. This enables Mercedes-Benz to identify trends and patterns, which can be used to improve its products and services.

5. **Improved product development:** By analyzing customer feedback and preferences, Mercedes-Benz can develop new products and features that better meet the needs of its customers. Schäfer notes that this approach has helped the company accelerate its product development process and bring innovations to market more quickly.

6. **Enhancing the customer experience:** The chatbot is integrated into the Mercedes me app, which provides a

seamless and convenient way for customers to interact with the company. Schäfer believes that this approach has enhanced the overall customer experience and contributed to increased brand loyalty.

7. **Collaboration with startup ecosystem:** Mercedes-Benz is collaborating with startups and other companies in the tech industry to stay at the forefront of AI innovation. Schäfer highlights that this approach has allowed the company to leverage the latest technologies and expertise to improve its products and services.

8. **Ethical considerations:** Schäfer emphasizes the importance of ethical considerations when using AI, particularly in areas like customer service and product development. Mercedes-Benz is committed to ensuring its use of AI is transparent, accountable, and respectful of customers' privacy and preferences.

You can see how Mercedes-Benz is leveraging the power of chatbots and AI to improve its customer service and product development. Using ChatGPT and analyzing real-time data, the company can provide personalized experiences for its customers, accelerate product development, and enhance brand loyalty.

Conclusion

Of course, there are more than just these three main areas where a business can be made for adoption of generative AI, but when tying it to marketing and the customer experience, these can be the most compelling ones. In the next chapter, we will move from the business case to some practical applications of generative AI for marketing teams.

Part 2:
Marketing Applications for Generative AI

With so many companies looking to adopt generative AI, it's important for marketing leaders to evaluate and understand the potential applications of this technology for their teams.

Over the next few chapters, we will explore the possible applications of generative AI in marketing from the perspective of marketing leaders who evaluate these tools and approaches for their teams. We will discuss topics such as what generative AI is, its benefits, potential use cases, and various tools available to adopt it. We will also explore the current market landscape, the challenges involved in implementing generative AI, and the potential opportunities that come with it.

Generative AI promises to revolutionize the way businesses approach their marketing strategies. Unlike other forms of AI, generative AI uses deep learning algorithms and neural networks to create fully original pieces of content, including text, images, music, and even videos. This allows for a highly personalized and targeted approach that traditional marketing techniques cannot compete with. For instance, generative AI can help businesses create unique product descriptions that cater to customer preferences, resulting in a more effective, targeted campaign.

Another potential application of generative AI is in automating the content creation process. Content creation can be time-consuming and requires a dedicated team of content writers. However, generative AI can help automate the process by generating ideas, crafting content, and even optimizing it for SEO. This can save companies a huge amount of time and money, allowing them to focus on other critical marketing tasks.

Generative AI can also help businesses to engage with their customers in more personalized and targeted ways. By using natural language processing, businesses can leverage the power of generative AI to craft unique and personalized responses to customer inquiries and comments, even in real time. This creates a seamless and highly personalized customer experience that can significantly improve customer satisfaction.

One of the challenges in adopting generative AI is selecting the right tool and framework to use. The market offers different options for businesses to adopt the technology, ranging from simple, pre-built models to more customizable frameworks that require skilled developers. Marketing leaders must weigh the costs and benefits of each option and choose the one that best aligns with their business goals and their team's capabilities.

As we have seen already, generative AI offers immense benefits for businesses and marketers, from enabling personalized content and automating content creation to improving customer engagement and satisfaction. However, before adopting generative AI, it's important for marketing leaders to understand the potential applications and challenges involved in implementing this technology. By doing so, they can make informed decisions that best align with their company's marketing goals and capabilities.

Let's keep going and explore the potential applications of generative AI in more detail over the next few chapters!

2.0 An Overview of Content Creation

As we explore the marketing applications of generative AI, we will start with perhaps the most obvious. Many marketers have gotten their introduction to generative AI through the realm of content creation. After all, the first time you used ChatGPT, did you ask it to write something, whether it was an article, a draft of a document for work, or something similar? Let's look at some ways that generative AI can help with content creation for marketers.

Written content

As a marketer, you know that creating compelling and engaging content is one of the most critical components of your marketing strategy. However, coming up with new ideas, writing first drafts, and improving your existing content are often challenging and time-consuming tasks.

Fortunately, with the rise of generative AI, marketers can now leverage automated tools to streamline the content creation process. In this article, we explore how generative AI can transform your content creation efforts by generating initial ideas, creating first drafts, improving existing content, and more.

Generating Initial Ideas

One of the most significant advantages of using generative AI for content creation is the ability to quickly generate many initial ideas. With the help of natural language processing and machine learning algorithms, generative AI tools can analyze data sets, identify themes, and generate relevant topics that can inspire your content creation efforts.

Creating First Drafts

Once you have generated initial ideas, generative AI can assist in creating first drafts by generating sentences or paragraphs that follow a particular style, voice, or tone. These tools can help you save time, effort, and resources, enabling you to focus on other critical aspects of creating a successful marketing campaign.

Improving or Adapting Existing Content

In addition to generating ideas and creating first drafts, generative AI can help you improve your existing content by suggesting new sentences, paragraphs, or even sections that can enhance the quality of your content. By analyzing and understanding your content's structure, generative AI tools can identify gaps, redundancies, and other areas of improvement that can boost your content's engagement and appeal.

Generative AI can greatly improve existing content by refining and transforming it to better suit specific purposes or tones based on a prompt. Here are some ways generative AI can be used to enhance existing content:

1. **Tone and Style:** Generative AI can be trained to mimic specific tones and styles based on a given prompt. For

example, if a brand wants to create social media posts that have a playful and lighthearted tone, the AI can be trained on examples of such content to generate new posts that fit the desired tone. This can help brands maintain a consistent voice across all their online channels.

2. **Sentence Structure:** Generative AI can also be used to correct awkward sentence structures or wording to make content more readable and engaging. For instance, if a piece of content has long, convoluted sentences, the AI can break them down into shorter, simpler ones that are easier to understand.

3. **Content Type:** One of the most powerful applications of generative AI in content creation is converting one type of content into another, for example, taking a long set of paragraphs and turning it into a marketing email or a social media post. The AI can analyze the existing content and generate new content that maintains the same message but in a different format, making it more versatile and effective across different channels.

4. **Length:** Generative AI can also be used to adjust content length to fit specific requirements. For instance, if a brand wants to create a series of social media posts that are all the same length, the AI can be trained to generate posts of a specific word count or character limit.

5. **Personalization:** Generative AI can also be used to personalize content based on specific audience segments or

individuals. By analyzing user data and behavior, the AI can generate content that speaks directly to the user's interests and needs, increasing engagement and conversion rates. We will talk a little more about this in the next section.

6. **Localization:** Finally, generative AI can be used to localize content for different markets and regions. By training the AI on examples of translated content, it can generate new content in different languages, making it easier for brands to expand their reach globally.

As you can see, generative AI has the potential to greatly improve existing content by refining tone, correcting sentence structure, converting one type of content into another, adjusting length, personalizing content, and localizing content for different markets. By leveraging these capabilities, brands can make their content more engaging, versatile, and effective across different channels, ultimately driving better results for their business.

Text transcriptions

Generative AI can revolutionize how we create and consume written content, especially when it comes to automatically transcribing speech within audio or video recordings. This technology can save teams hours and provide them with valuable transcriptions of meetings, speeches, and other important events. Here are some potential use cases for generative AI in creating written content from audio and video recordings:

1. **Meeting Notes:** With the ability to automatically transcribe audio recordings, teams can save time and effort by having

quicker notes for meetings. This can be especially useful for remote meetings where taking detailed notes manually may not be feasible. Generative AI can help ensure that important details are captured accurately and promptly.

2. **Speech Transcriptions:** Generative AI can also be used to transcribe speeches, lectures, and other audio recordings accurately. This can provide valuable written content for archival purposes or distribution to a wider audience. For example, a speaker may want to publish their speech online or in print, and generative AI can help make this process more efficient and cost-effective.

3. **Interviews and Testimonials:** In addition to meetings and speeches, generative AI can be used to transcribe audio recordings of interviews and testimonials. This can provide valuable insights and quotes for marketing materials, press releases, or other written content.

4. **Podcast and Video Transcripts:** With the rise of podcasts and videos, generative AI can help automate the process of creating transcripts for these formats. This can provide a more accessible way for audiences to engage with the content, especially for those who may prefer to read rather than watch or listen.

5. **Research and Analysis:** Generative AI can also be used to analyze audio recordings and extract valuable insights, such as sentiment analysis or topic modeling. This can provide a more

efficient way to conduct research and analysis, especially for large datasets.

6. **New Content Based on Audio:** Finally, generative AI can be used to create new written content based on the transcripts of audio or video recordings. For example, a team may want to use a speech transcript as a starting point for a blog post or article, and generative AI can help refine and expand upon the content.

Benefits of text generation

Generative AI tools are a cost-effective and scalable way to produce high-quality content on a large scale. With the ability to automate many aspects of the content creation process, marketers can produce more content in less time and at a lower cost than traditional methods. This scalability can be especially useful for companies that operate in multiple languages, geographies, or target markets.

Thus, generative AI for text generation is a game-changer for marketers looking to streamline their text-based content creation process. From generating initial ideas to creating first drafts, improving existing content, personalization, localization, and scalability, generative AI tools can help you create engaging, high-quality content that resonates with your target audience. As CMOs and marketing leaders, now is the time to start incorporating generative AI tools into your content creation strategy to stay ahead of the competition and foster stronger customer relationships.

Visual content

Whether you're creating a social media post, an advertisement, or a website, the right visual can make all the difference. However, as you well know, creating visuals can be a time-consuming process that requires a lot of skill and creativity. This is where generative AI comes in. With the help of generative AI, marketers can now easily create high-quality visual content in a matter of minutes.

You'll notice similarities here between how imagery can leverage generative AI and how text-based content can, so we will be spending a little less time on each of these aspects. Even so, let's discuss how generative AI can be used by marketers to create visual content.

Generating Rough Drafts of Image Concepts

One of the ways marketers can use generative AI is by generating rough drafts of image concepts. With the help of generative AI, marketers can quickly create a range of different concepts for an image, allowing them to narrow down and refine ideas quickly. This can save marketers a lot of time and effort and can result in more innovative visual content.

Creating First Drafts of Photographic Images or Illustrations

Another way generative AI can help marketers is by creating first drafts of photographic images or illustrations. This can be especially useful when time is limited and a marketer needs to create content quickly. With the help of generative AI, marketers can get a head start on the creative process, allowing them to focus on refining the content rather than starting from scratch.

Improving Existing Imagery

Much the same way that generative AI is able to improve existing text content, it can also help marketers improve existing imagery. By analyzing an image with AI technology, marketers can identify areas that need improvement, such as brightness, color balance, contrast, and more. This can result in more professional-looking visuals sure to grab the attention of your target audience.

Automating the Process

Finally, generative AI can help automate the process of creating visual content. By using generative AI, marketers can quickly and easily create various visuals without the need for human input. This can save marketers time and money, resulting in more consistent visual content that is more likely to generate engagement.

Generative AI is revolutionizing the way marketers create visual content. Using generative AI, marketers can quickly and easily create high-quality visuals, saving time and effort. Whether you're generating rough drafts of image concepts, creating first drafts of photographic images or illustrations, improving existing imagery, or automating the process of creating visual content, generative AI can transform how you approach visual content creation.

Videos, audio, music, and more

Of course, there are many more applications for generative AI, and certainly more popping up each day. For instance, it can potentially revolutionize how video, audio, and music content is created and consumed. In the realm of video content, generative AI can be used to generate entire videos or just certain elements such as backgrounds, characters, or special effects. For example, a brand could use generative AI to create an animated commercial that showcases their product in action. The AI could generate the background, characters, and special effects based on the brand's specifications, saving time and resources compared to traditional animation methods.

When it comes to audio content, generative AI can be used to generate speech in both original languages as well as translated languages. This technology has significant implications for language translation, allowing for more accurate and natural-sounding translations. Additionally, generative AI can be used to create original music that can be used in advertisements, promotional videos, and other forms of media. This could involve generating entire musical compositions or just specific elements such as melodies or beats.

In the world of music, generative AI is already being used to create original compositions. For example, the music streaming service Amper Music uses an AI-powered composition tool that allows users to select a style and mood for their desired track and then generates the entire composition based on that input. This technology has the potential to democratize music creation, allowing anyone with access to a computer to create professional-sounding tracks without the need for extensive musical training or expensive equipment.

Finally, why stop at creating just one part of a piece of marketing collateral, such as a text headline, a key image, or the like? Generative AI tools can also pull several pieces together—combinations of text and images—to create designs and layouts. This has immediate potential to be used in digital scenarios, such as creating multiple variations for user experience (UX) design for things like landing pages or mobile app screens or in print-based scenarios like direct mail, print ads, or brochures.

Real-time personalization across the customer journey

While it includes text and images, the last category of content we will look at is the most comprehensive and powerful. This is also a case where generative AI can meaningfully be paired with other types of AI tools, such as predictive analytics, to turbocharge its effects.

Creating a personalized buyer's journey is crucial for businesses to stand out from the competition and build long-term customer relationships. By leveraging generative AI and predictive analytics together, businesses can create a more tailored experience for their customers at every stage of the journey, from awareness to post-purchase loyalty. In this article, we will explore how these technologies can work together to provide personalized content, offers, and experiences at the right time and on the right channel.

Awareness Stage: Generating Personalized Content

At the awareness stage, generative AI can help businesses generate personalized content that speaks directly to customers' needs and interests. By analyzing customer data and behavior, predictive analytics can identify patterns and trends that indicate what a customer is likely to be interested in.

Generative AI can then be used to create customized content, such as product descriptions, blog posts, or social media updates, tailored to the customer's preferences. This helps to capture the customer's attention, build brand awareness, and establish a relationship with the customer.

Consideration Stage: Creating Personalized Offers

As the customer moves into the consideration stage, generative AI can help businesses create personalized offers tailored to their specific needs and preferences. By analyzing customer data and behavior, predictive analytics can identify patterns and trends that indicate what a customer will likely do next.

Generative AI can then be used to create customized offers, such as discounts, free trials, or special promotions, designed to incentivize the customer to take action. This helps to move the customer closer to a purchase decision and increases the likelihood of conversion.

Purchase Stage: Providing Personalized Experiences

At the purchase stage, generative AI can help businesses provide personalized experiences that make customers feel valued and appreciated.

By analyzing customer data and behavior, predictive analytics can identify patterns and trends that indicate what a customer will likely do next.

Generative AI can then be used to create customized experiences, such as personalized product recommendations or upsells/cross-sells, that are tailored to the customer's preferences. This helps to increase the average order value, improve customer satisfaction, and build long-term loyalty.

Post-Purchase Stage: Enhancing Customer Retention

Finally, at the post-purchase stage, generative AI can help businesses enhance customer retention by providing personalized content, offers, and experiences that keep the customer engaged and satisfied. By analyzing customer data and behavior, predictive analytics can identify patterns and trends that indicate what a customer will likely do next.

Generative AI can then be used to create customized experiences, such as follow-up emails or personalized product recommendations, that are tailored to the customer's preferences. This helps to increase customer retention, build brand loyalty, and drive repeat business.

By leveraging generative AI and predictive analytics together, businesses can create a more personalized buyer's journey that reaches customers at all stages, from awareness to post-purchase loyalty. Businesses can build trust, establish relationships, and drive long-term growth and success by providing personalized content, offers, and experiences at the right time and on the right channel. As technology continues to evolve, it is essential for businesses to stay ahead of the curve and leverage these innovations to create a more personalized and engaging experience for their customers.

Conclusion

As we've explored in this chapter, generative AI has the potential to revolutionize the way marketers create and manage content. From text-based content, like social media posts and blog articles, to image-based content, like graphics and product photos, to video and audio content, like ads and podcasts, generative AI can help streamline the content creation process and improve the overall quality of the content. Generative AI can also be used to create designs and layouts for websites, emails, and other marketing materials.

But the potential applications of generative AI don't stop there. In the next chapter, we'll explore how generative AI can assist with personalizing the customer experience. By analyzing customer data and behavior, generative AI can help marketers create customized content, offers, and recommendations tailored to each individual customer. This can lead to higher engagement rates, increased customer loyalty, and, ultimately, increased sales and revenue.

2.1 Additive Functionality for Existing Tools

As the capabilities of generative AI continue to expand and become more accessible, marketers are increasingly faced with a decision: when should they use standalone generative AI tools versus leveraging these features within existing applications? Both approaches have advantages and disadvantages, and understanding these factors is crucial for marketers to make informed decisions and achieve their desired results.

Standalone Generative AI Tools

Let's start by discussing the potential benefits of using standalone generative AI tools, whether that is something like Jasper for content creation, DALL-E or Midjourney for image generation, or SwellAI for generating text content from audio, or many more examples. There are a few factors to consider here:

1. Specialized functionality: Standalone generative AI tools are often designed with a specific use case or task in mind, providing more focused and advanced features compared to those within existing applications. For example, some text generation tools specifically built for generative AI may

perform better than multi-purpose applications with generative AI functionality "bolted" on, though, of course, this comes with a very big caveat that it depends greatly on the platform.

2. Greater customization: Standalone tools typically offer more extensive customization options, allowing marketers to tailor the AI-generated output to their specific branding, tone, and style. This is particularly important when creating high-volume content or seeking unique creative ideas beyond what the tool's default settings can provide.

3. Flexibility in integration: Standalone generative AI tools can be integrated into existing workflows and platforms, allowing marketers to incorporate AI-generated content into their marketing strategies without being limited by the capabilities of a single application.

Existing Applications with Generative AI Capabilities

Now, let's move to talking about existing applications that have incorporated generative AI features into their existing capabilities. I'd venture to say that there aren't many web-based applications that aren't at least considering this—if they haven't rolled out new features already. There are a few factors to consider here when deciding whether to utilize an existing platform as opposed to a standalone tool that specializes in generative AI:

1. **Familiarity and convenience:** Marketers already using Adobe Photoshop, Hubspot, or other popular applications can leverage generative AI features within these tools, eliminating the need to learn new software and interfaces. This familiarity and convenience can speed up the content creation process and reduce the risk of errors or missteps.

2. **Seamless integration:** Incorporating generative AI capabilities within existing applications often results in a more streamlined workflow, as marketers can access these features without switching between multiple tools. This integration can lead to increased productivity and efficiency.

3. **Strength of features:** While a tool you know and love may now suddenly have generative AI features, how robust and flexible are they? Is the most compelling reason to use it simply because you are already *in* the application, or does the generative capability stand up on its own?

4. **Continuous improvement:** That said, as these existing tools continuously update and improve their generative AI features, marketers using these tools can benefit from these advancements without needing to switch to a new standalone tool.

Factors to Consider for Marketers

So, as you take these options into account, here are a few ways to look at a comparison between standalone generative AI tools and using existing platforms that have integrated generative AI features:

1. Task-specific requirements: Assess the specific needs of each marketing task or project. If a standalone generative AI tool offers more specialized functionality, it may be the better choice. However, using the integrated generative AI might be more convenient and efficient if the task can be accomplished with the existing application's features.

2. Customization needs: Evaluate the level of customization required for the content being generated. A standalone tool may be more suitable if unique branding or creative elements are necessary. However, if generic templates or styles are acceptable, the integrated generative AI within an existing application might meet the marketer's needs.

3. Workflow integration: Consider the compatibility and integration with other tools and platforms used by the marketing team. If seamless integration is essential, using the generative AI features within an existing application may be the better choice.

4. Cost and investment: Standalone generative AI tools may require additional licensing fees or upfront costs, while integrated features within existing applications are often

included in the standard subscription or license fee. Marketers should consider these financial factors when deciding which approach to take.

Marketers need to carefully assess their specific requirements and goals when deciding whether to use standalone generative AI tools or leverage the capabilities within existing applications. Both approaches have advantages and disadvantages, and understanding these factors is crucial for achieving desired results in marketing efforts. By taking the time to evaluate the task at hand, customization needs, workflow integration, and cost considerations, marketers can make informed decisions that help them achieve their objectives effectively and efficiently.

2.2 Some Tips for Better AI-Generated Content

Now that we've explored several types of content that can be created with generative AI tools, let's talk through some tips to make the most of these tools and go beyond the basics.

Let's start with creating a good prompt

As a marketing team member, you know the importance of creating compelling content that resonates with your target audience. With generative AI tools like text generation, image synthesis, and video creation, you can take your content to the next level by leveraging the power of artificial intelligence. However, to get the most out of these tools, it's essential to craft effective prompts that guide the AI in producing the desired output.

Here's how to create great prompts for generative AI in marketing.

1. **Define Your Objective:** Before creating a prompt, you need to determine the purpose of your AI-generated content. Are you looking to increase engagement, drive conversions, or enhance brand awareness? Knowing your objective will help you tailor your prompt to achieve the desired outcome.

2. **Use Specific Language:** Avoid vague language and instead use specific terms that convey the tone, style, and messaging you desire. For instance, if you're looking to create a humorous video, use words like "witty," "quirky," or "lighthearted" in your prompt.

3. **Provide Context:** Give the AI as much context as possible about the content you want to generate. This can include references to existing marketing materials, customer personas of both the speaker or author or of the intended audience, or industry trends that would be helpful to highlight within. The more information you provide, the better the AI can tailor its output to your needs.

4. **Use Templates:** To streamline the process and ensure consistency, consider using templates for your prompts. For example, if you're creating a series of social media posts, develop a template with the necessary information like hashtags, tone, and style.

5. **Provide Examples:** Include examples of the type of content you want the AI to generate. For instance, if you're creating a video script, provide a sample script or storyboard to guide the AI in producing similar content.

6. **Test and Refine:** As with any marketing strategy, it's essential to test and refine your prompts based on the results you achieve. Analyze the output of your generative AI tools and adjust your prompts accordingly to optimize their

performance.

Don't be afraid to ask the AI to refine or clarify something, either. Many chat interfaces allow this and, in some cases, encourage it to get better, or at the very least, better at giving you the kind of content you seek!

Some Examples of Effective Prompts

1. **For a social media campaign:** "Create a series of 6 humorous videos (30 seconds each) showcasing our new product, emphasizing its unique features and appeal to a young adult audience."

2. **For an email marketing campaign:** "Write a set of 5 email newsletters (subject lines, copy, and calls-to-action included) targeting our existing customer base with personalized offers based on their past purchases."

3. **For a content marketing strategy:** "Generate 10 blog post ideas (500 words each) focused on our industry's latest trends and tips for improving our customers' experiences while maintaining a conversational tone and including relevant keywords."

4. **For an influencer marketing campaign:** "Create a list of 20 social media posts (images/videos and captions) featuring our brand ambassadors showcasing our product in various scenarios, with a mix of serious and humorous tones to engage their followers."

5. **For a video advertisement:** "Develop a script for a 30-second video ad showcasing our new product's key features, benefits, and unique selling points, with a focus on emotional storytelling and a memorable call-to-action."

Of course, part of the fun of generative AI is coming up with your approaches and prompts that get you the best results, so try these, but also experiment to see what works best for you and your teams' needs.

Creating better AI-generated blog content

Creating engaging and informative blog content is essential to any successful marketing strategy. However, coming up with fresh ideas and writing interesting blog posts can be challenging. This is where generative AI comes in.

Generative AI is an innovative technology that uses algorithms to create unique and original content. It reduces time spent by writers, provides consistency, saves time, and increases efficiency. Let's explore how to use generative AI to create customized blog content while still maintaining control of your brand's voice.

Understand Your Brand Voice

The first step in creating customized blog content through generative AI is understanding your brand's voice. Establishing an authentic voice for your brand will ensure that your communication is consistent across all channels.

It's important to identify the tone, voice, and emotions your brand should project to the audience. Once you've identified your brand voice, you can create templates to guide the AI content creation process. The templates will guide the AI to maintain your brand's voice.

Choose a Reputable Generative AI Program

The second step is to choose a reputable generative AI program that matches your brand's needs. There are several AI-powered content creation tools in the market. Choosing a program that can produce high-quality and authentic content is essential while ensuring consistency with your brand's voice.

The program's customization features, including tone, language, tone, and formatting, should be easily adjustable. Additionally, ensure that your chosen program complies with GDPR and other data privacy regulations.

Train the Generative AI

The third step is to provide extensive training and testing of the generative AI to understand your brand's specific language and tone. You can feed the AI with relevant content and data, including previous blog posts and website copy. The generative AI program should learn from this data to understand your brand's preferred tone and language. You can also provide the AI with specific keywords to include in the content to ensure search engine optimization.

Edit and Publish with Human Oversight

Although generative AI produces high-quality and authentic content, it's essential to have a human touch. Before publishing the content, you must edit it to ensure it matches your brand's voice. You can use a content editor or a copywriter to make the necessary changes. Additionally, ensure that the AI-generated content is fact-checked to avoid errors and inaccuracies.

Monitor the Analytics

The last and vital step is to monitor the AI-generated content's analytics. You can then track and analyze the blog performance, such as page views, click-throughs, and engagement levels, to measure the content's effectiveness. You can use this data to optimize and adjust your brand's voice and the AI's settings to improve the blog content's quality.

As you can see, generative AI can be incredibly helpful in creating customized blog content while still maintaining control of your brand's voice. It saves time, increases efficiency, and ensures consistency in your communication. Ensure you understand your brand voice, choose a reputable generative AI program, train the AI, edit and publish with human oversight, and monitor analytics. With these steps, you can create high-quality, authentic content that resonates with your audience.

Generating Better Campaign Ideas

In today's day and age, marketing campaigns have become more advanced than ever. From social media and email campaigns to webinars and podcasts, marketers have to develop innovative ways to keep their audience engaged.

But in the quest to stand out from the crowd, it's easy to overlook the importance of adhering to brand standards and targeting your desired audience. This is where generative AI comes in. In this blog post, we'll explore how you can leverage generative AI to generate different marketing campaign ideas, headlines, and descriptions while still focusing on your target audience and adhering to brand standards.

Understanding What Generative AI Is Good At—and what it isn't good at

Before diving into how generative AI can benefit your marketing campaigns, let's define it. Generative AI uses data and algorithms to create new content based on set parameters. Essentially, it "thinks" like a human but can generate far more ideas than anyone can. The tool learns from the data it receives and uses that knowledge to create new content. In other words, it's like having an assistant who can come up with infinite campaign ideas.

Set the right parameters

Implementing generative AI into your marketing campaigns is easier than you might think. First, you'll need to identify the parameters you want the tool to work within. This includes your brand's voice, target audience, and other important factors in your campaigns. Your AI tool will then work within those parameters to generate various creative ideas.

Embrace the variety

One of the primary advantages of generative AI is the sheer amount of ideas it can come up with. This is especially helpful in brainstorming sessions where you want to explore as many ideas as possible.

Additionally, generative AI eliminates the bias that humans naturally bring to the table. It doesn't have prior experiences or emotions that might prevent it from exploring new and innovative ideas. Finally, generative AI is highly efficient, helping to save marketers time and resources that would otherwise be spent on generating various campaign ideas.

Pay Attention to Your Brand Standards & Audience Preferences

Of course, while generative AI can come up with endless campaign ideas, it's still crucial to adhere to your brand's standards and reach your desired audience. The right AI tool will be able to learn your brand's tone and target a specific audience with each campaign, but it will take some training and time. Doing so ensures your campaigns remain consistent with your brand's vision and resonate with your intended audience.

You can create truly powerful marketing campaigns by using generative AI to generate new campaign ideas, headlines, and descriptions. With more ideas than ever before, you can hone in on the ones that resonate most with your audience. What's more, your marketing campaigns will remain true to your brand's vision, helping to establish your brand identity with your audience.

Conclusion

Leveraging the power of generative AI can be the difference between a successful campaign and one that falls flat. By allowing AI to generate new ideas, concepts, and content, you can expand your campaigns' creative horizons while still adhering to your brand standards and targeting your desired audience. In the next section, we will go a bit deeper in exploring how to integrate generative AI into the work you and your teams do.

Part 3:
Generative AI in Practice

In this final section of our book on generative AI, we will explore the practical applications of generative AI in the real world. We will discuss choosing a winning philosophy for AI adoption, what to watch out for when adopting AI within your marketing team, and the best way to integrate Generative AI into your existing teams, processes, and platforms.

By the end of this section, you will have a solid understanding of leveraging generative AI to improve your marketing operations and achieve your goals.

Let's keep moving forward!

3.1 Picking a winning AI philosophy

With all the hype around AI these days, it may feel like there is no time to step back and consider some of the deeper implications of its adoption. After all, who wants to be the last to get on the bandwagon, particularly when AI, unlike some other recent much-hyped areas (I'm looking at you, metaverse and NFTs) adopting artificial intelligence-based tools and platforms can offer some immediate benefits to organizations?

That said, I want to make the argument that your organization needs an "AI philosophy," and quickly. It is likely already too late to pause adoption by your teams, but you can still establish an enterprise-wide stance on its adoption and best practices. This will enable you to operationalize AI more easily and to more clearly articulate your AI vision to your employees, partners, and customers.

To help you create an AI philosophy, I will walk through a few scenarios, and then we'll end with a recommendation. So, to start, let's talk through three overall approaches and explore the pros and cons of each.

Friend/Foe

The first scenario of our exploration of AI philosophies is perhaps the most extreme. I call this Friend or Foe. There are two potential cases here:

- **Executives and leaders love AI** because they believe it will cut costs, jobs, and overhead in general, and employees hate it because they fear for their jobs, or

- **Employees love AI** because it saves them time and helps them avoid the drudgery of their work, and executives and leaders hate it because they are concerned about risks, employees who aren't fully utilized, and the nagging feeling that they are losing human productivity and quality.

For many, this might sound familiar, as artificial intelligence seems to be a polarizing topic, with viewpoints varying greatly and depending on who within an organization you are talking to and their role. Let's look at the pros and cons of this friend or foe approach.

Pros

In full transparency, there aren't too many pros here to discuss. We've essentially got leaders and managers against employees, which is never a good setup. Still, let's talk through a few here, as these points will become more relevant as we explore the frenemy and partner relationships.

However, the pro of considering AI a friend is that there is an openness to using it and a willingness to look past some obstacles and on the bright side of adoption. There is also a willingness to try a few tools and platforms to see the best one for each application.

The pro of considering AI a *foe* is a more cautious approach in an as-yet unregulated environment with many gray areas. That said, I think foe is a pretty extreme term here, which is why the next scenario looks at AI as a *frenemy* instead. However, some big ethical issues need to be looked at, and some industries can have much bigger negative repercussions for not taking into account bias, copyright infringement, or other issues.

That said, if roughly half of the organization considers AI either a friend or foe, it is hard to have a productive dialogue about some of the pros of either way of thinking, so organizations that find themselves in a friend or foe situation may not be able to benefit from the pros here fully.

Cons

Similarly, the cons of this friend or foe approach is that no one "side" really wins in this scenario. There is distrust on one side or the other of the leadership/employee divide, depending on who treats AI as "friend," and instead of real dialogue about the benefits and drawbacks, there are sides in a battle.

Overall, the friend or foe approach is much too binary to work in the real world. Organizations taking this view are not likely to succeed in the long run; they will quickly (if they haven't already) run into some serious issues and internal disconnects, which will likely spill over into their customer communications and interactions soon enough.

In the best case, these companies will miss out on opportunities to innovate and embrace some of the wide-reaching benefits of AI-based tools, methods, and platforms. They might overlook some of the risks and dangers because there are factions in place of a realistic and productive dialogue.

Frenemy

This brings us to the next type of AI philosophy: the frenemy. This is where the enterprise is cautiously optimistic, and, depending on the specifics, AI can either be a friend or enemy and often a little of each, even within the same teams, roles, and areas of the business. Though this may seem like a paradox, in some ways, this is the most realistic philosophy because it acknowledges there are both upsides and downsides.

As I mentioned in the previous section on friend or foe, there are real opportunities but also real potential conflicts and issues that enterprises within all industries need to consider. Thus, this parallel approach can make sense. Let's explore some of the pros and cons here.

Pros

The frenemy approach allows organizations to have a more nuanced relationship with AI. In some ways, it may be beneficial to different teams and roles within the organization, yet in others, it may require more caution and even a pause before implementing anything.

While it may seem contradictory, treating AI as a frenemy can help organizations take small steps towards greater AI adoption without blindly opening the floodgates and reaping whatever that may bring.

Cons

Those pros aside, using a term like "frenemy" implies some skepticism and an assumption that there are pure negatives to deeper AI adoption rather than areas that simply need some governance and guardrails. While these may be justified, it would be better to approach this in a more open way that can still acknowledge ethical, compliance, regulatory, or other concerns.

Thus, the cons of a frenemy philosophy are that there may not be an openness to experimentation and innovation in some key areas, and those blind spots may hinder bigger growth in areas that competitors could exploit as a weakness.

Partner

Finally, we get to the most symbiotic of the three relationships between businesses and AI: the partnership philosophy. At its essence, the partner philosophy of AI adoption means being realistic about the potential risk areas while working with AI to innovate and find what works and what doesn't.

When we think of a good partner, it also implies several things:

- Good partners have a transparent relationship, and there is open communication between them.

- Good partners take the good with the bad and can make compromises that still reap benefits.

- Good partners are able to give and take without sacrificing the relationship and while striving for a win-win.

- Good partners understand what each is great at and can adapt how they work to maximize benefits and outcomes accordingly.

Let's look at some of the pros and cons of a partnership approach.

Pros

The biggest benefit of the partner philosophy is that, from my perspective, it sets up the enterprise for the most productive long-term relationship with AI and the benefits and cautions it brings. In a partnership philosophy, there are no good or bad assumptions, but more simply, an understanding that every benefit must be balanced with the risks and uncertainties.

As AI assistants, applications, and other platforms become more conversational and require less technical knowledge to operate, a partner philosophy also "humanizes" the relationship between software and the people who use it. While this benefits the teams using it by democratizing access to features and functionality previously hidden behind layers of coding and well-formatted requests, it also benefits their customers.

After all, instead of software being a blunt tool to be used in the service of providing something to customers, with AI as a *partner,* there is a sense that teams and artificial intelligence can work together towards a common goal of providing a great customer experience, each learning from the other continually over time.

Cons

While there are a lot of pros here, the caution in this approach is to look at the relationship between AI and the enterprise with a little too rosy a view. After all, as much as we might want to consider AI part of the team, it's zeroes and ones, not actual people!

While the partnership philosophy might be a little more idealistic than the frenemy approach, and definitely more so than the friend or foe approach can be, exploring a relationship with AI that looks at it as a partner that augments and enables your human teams to do more, extend their reach, and understand and serve customers better can be a win-win scenario for the business and your customers.

Conclusion

As you can see, there is more than one approach you and your organization can take in setting the foundation for a relationship with AI and AI-based tools and platforms. While I don't recommend the friend or foe or frenemy approaches per se, there are aspects of each that you should consider so as not to get blinded by the shiny object of the moment: artificial intelligence.

That said, looking at AI as a partner for your organization is an area I would highly recommend you explore further. There are plenty of reasons to be cautious about AI adoption. Still, there are just as many (if not more) reasons to be optimistic about the benefits it can bring to your business, your employees, and your customers.

3.2 Things to Watch Out For

Of course, generative AI in practice is not without its potential challenges and things to watch out for. There are quite a few here, so let's group them into a few categories that we will discuss in more detail, one at a time:

- Time and quality
- Garbage in, garbage out
- Legal and regulatory
- Brands that work with external agencies and contractors

Let's spend some time discussing each of these in more depth.

Time & Quality

While generative AI can be a powerful tool for marketers, there are several potential pitfalls to watch out for when adopting this technology. Here are some things to keep in mind:

Using Generative AI as a Starting Point

One common mistake is to rely too heavily on generative AI as a starting point for idea generation and first drafts. While AI can generate many ideas quickly, it's important to remember that these ideas may not always be the best or most relevant ones. It's important to review and refine AI-generated output to ensure it meets your brand's standards and objectives.

Impact on Hiring and Workflow

Generative AI may affect how you hire new marketing roles and current team members' work. For example, if AI can generate content quickly and accurately, you may need to rethink your hiring strategy or adjust the workload of your team members. It's important to consider these implications and plan accordingly.

AI Hallucinations

Another potential issue with generative AI is the problem of "AI hallucinations." This occurs when the AI introduces inaccurate information or data into the work it generates. For example, an AI might generate a piece of content that includes a fictional product or service, or it might misinterpret the intent of a campaign. This happened to me as I was preparing for a keynote at a conference just recently. I asked a generative AI tool to write a bio for me, and it invented a company that never existed and said I was its former CEO!

Thus, it's important to carefully review and fact-check AI-generated output to avoid these types of errors.

Maintaining Brand Consistency

Finally, it's important to be careful about maintaining brand consistency when working with AI-generated output. Suppose you're using generative AI to create content or messaging for multiple channels. In that case, it's essential to ensure that the output is consistent across all channels and aligns with your brand's overall identity and values. This may require careful review and editing of AI-generated output to ensure it meets your standards.

Overall, while generative AI can be a powerful tool for marketers, it's important to be aware of these potential pitfalls and take steps to mitigate them. By carefully reviewing and fact-checking AI-generated output, maintaining brand consistency, and considering the impact on hiring and workflow, you can ensure that your use of generative AI is successful and effective.

Garbage in, Garbage Out

This term (and its acronym, GIGO) has been around for a while, but never more important than in an AI-driven world.

Data Quality Matters

The quality of the data sources you use to train your generative AI models matters greatly. If the training data is noisy, biased, or incomplete, the resulting models may perform poorly or even perpetuate existing biases. For example, if a language model is trained on a dataset containing derogatory language or stereotypes, it may generate similar language or reinforce those stereotypes. Therefore, it's essential to carefully curate your training data and ensure it is representative of the population you are trying to serve.

Ethical Considerations:

Generative AI models can perpetuate biases and reinforce existing social inequalities if not designed with ethical considerations in mind. For example, a language model that generates job descriptions may inadvertently exclude certain groups of people if it is trained on biased data. Similarly, an image generator that creates images of people may perpetuate stereotypes or reinforce harmful gender or racial biases. Therefore, it's essential to consider the ethical implications of your generative AI models and take steps to mitigate any potential biases.

I asked Tara DeZao of Pega to elaborate on these ethical considerations, and here's what she had to say:

> *"Similar to any technology innovation that has come before, AI carries big risks with it. That includes things like bias when using data inputs on demographic data like ethnicity, age, and gender. When we're examining processes that impact humans greatly, like credit scoring, employee recruitment, etc., this is very dangerous, especially if the algorithm is opaque and the organization can't explain why the AI made a certain decision. This opens organizations up to serious legal consequences.*
>
> *Organizations can inadvertently exacerbate existing bias. AI algorithms are reliant on the data we feed into them, and much of the data on the internet specifically reflects the bias and discrimination in society. When you layer on generative AI, we start seeing things like representational harms, the representation of groups and individuals with stereotypical or discriminatory*

language or imagery. For example, a majority of CEOs in the U.S. are white males. According to the Society of Human Resource Management, data from 2019 reflected that 85.6% of Fortune 500 CEOs were White men[20]. That means that if Dall-e or Midjourney is prompted to create an image of a CEO with non-specific gender language, it will almost certainly return an image of a white man. So a marketer will then have produced creative that is biased and then, if it were put into production, added to the existing digital cannon of already biased images, reinforcing bias over and over again.

The good news is that if organizations have the right human oversight and are committed to transparency, they can use GenAI to understand AI-powered decisioning and know exactly how decisions are made and not present content or offers to their customers that contain bias.

Or be able to explain it to regulators, etc. The more marketers we have that are committed to responsible AI, the less these technologies will be used to create harm, even when unintentional."

Organizations need to take note and take proactive measures here, and not simply wait for governments to regulate, as they can be slow to do so.

Additional considerations

In addition to these two key watch-outs, there are several other potential issues to be aware of when adopting generative AI, including:

- **Overfitting:** Generative AI models can easily overfit the training data, which means they become too specialized to the training data and fail to generalize well to new, unseen data. This can result in poor performance on real-world data. To avoid overfitting, it's essential to use techniques like regularization, early stopping, or ensembling multiple models.

- **Lack of interpretability:** Generative AI models can be difficult to interpret, making it challenging to understand why the model makes certain predictions or generates certain outputs. This lack of transparency can make it difficult to identify and address issues with the model. To address this, it's essential to use techniques like feature importance or visualizations to gain insights into how the model works.

- **Potential for misuse:** Generative AI models can be used maliciously, such as creating convincing fake news articles or deepfakes. Therefore, it's essential to consider the potential risks and benefits of your generative AI models and take steps to mitigate any potential misuse.

While generative AI offers tremendous opportunities for marketers, it's important to be aware of these potential watch-outs and take steps to mitigate them. By carefully curating your training data, considering ethical implications, avoiding overfitting, increasing interpretability, and being mindful of the potential for misuse, you can ensure that your generative AI models are effective, responsible, and successful.

Legal & Regulatory

As with any emerging technology, marketers must be aware of several legal and regulatory considerations when adopting generative AI. These include intellectual property considerations and ever-evolving regulations on AI usage, data privacy, and other areas that affect generative AI usage.

Intellectual Property Considerations

Generative AI models can create new and original content, such as images, videos, music, and text. This raises important questions about who owns the intellectual property rights to this content. In some cases, the AI model itself may be considered the author of the content it generates, while in other cases, the person or organization that trained the model may be seen as the owner.

Marketers must be aware of these legal considerations and ensure they have the necessary permissions and clearances to use any copyrighted or trademarked materials in their generative AI projects. They should also be mindful of the potential for their own content to be copied or misused by others and take steps to protect their intellectual property.

2. Ever-Evolving Regulations on AI Usage:

The use of AI is subject to various regulations, including data privacy laws, anti-discrimination laws, and consumer protection laws. These regulations are constantly evolving, and marketers must be aware of any changes affecting their generative AI projects.

For example, the European Union (EU) and its General Data Protection Regulation (GDPR), first initiated in May 2018[21], gives consumers certain rights, such as the right to access, correct, or delete their personal data. Marketers using generative AI must ensure that they comply with these regulations and respect their customers' privacy rights.

Along these lines, but more specific to artificial intelligence, in April 2021, the EU proposed the first regulatory framework for AI, called the AI Act[22]. This framework addresses four areas, or "obligations," that consist of the following:

- Unacceptable risks, which include things like cognitive behavioral manipulation of vulnerable populations and real-time biometric identification systems
- High risks, which would deal with AI systems used in vehicles, medical devices, and toys (among other items)
- Generative AI, which will need to comply with transparency requirements about how content is generated and the sources of information to prevent copyright infringement
- Limited risks that include systems that might manipulate images, audio, and video that might create deepfakes and similar outputs.

Europe is not alone, either. As of writing this book, Canada is considering a similar proposal to the EU's, called the Artificial Intelligence and Data Act[23], the United States drafted the Blueprint for an AI Bill of Rights in October 2022[24], and China's regulations went into effect August 15, 2023[25].

In addition to country or region-specific regulations, there may be other specific regulations around the use of AI in certain industries, such as healthcare or finance. Marketers must be aware of relevant regulations and ensure their generative AI projects are compliant.

Data Privacy Considerations

Generative AI models often rely on large amounts of data to function effectively. This data may include personal information, such as names, addresses, or other identifiable details. Marketers must be aware of their obligations under data privacy laws and ensure that they are protecting the privacy of their customers.

These laws would include the EU's GDPR regulations we just discussed and any others that might apply depending on where the company operates. The United States has a few, including California's, as well as other state-specific laws and regulations, and there are many others for other countries worldwide.

One approach to mitigate risk with consumer data privacy issues is to use de-identified or anonymized data, which removes any personally identifiable information from the dataset. This can help to mitigate the risk of data breaches and other privacy violations.

Bias and Discrimination

Generative AI models can perpetuate biases and discrimination if trained on biased or incomplete data. Marketers must be aware of these risks and take steps to ensure that their generative AI models are fair and unbiased.

One approach is to use diverse and representative training data, which can help mitigate the risk of bias and discrimination. Additionally, marketers should regularly monitor their generative AI models for any signs of bias or discrimination and take steps to address these issues if they arise.

Transparency and Explainability

As with any AI model, it is important that generative AI models are transparent and explainable. Marketers must be able to understand how their generative AI models work and why they produce certain outputs. This can help build trust in the technology and ensure it is used responsibly.

To achieve transparency and explainability, marketers can use techniques such as feature importance analysis or visualizations to gain insights into how their generative AI models work. Additionally, they should be prepared to explain their AI-generated content if regulators or customers request it.

There are several legal and regulatory considerations that marketers must be aware of when adopting generative AI. These include intellectual property considerations, ever-evolving regulations on AI usage, data privacy concerns, bias and discrimination, and transparency and explainability. By understanding these issues and taking steps to address them, marketers can ensure that their generative AI projects are successful and responsible.

Brands that work with external agencies and contractors

 Companies that hire external marketing agencies to create content using generative AI technologies such as machine learning and natural language processing (NLP) should take several considerations to protect themselves from potential intellectual property, data privacy, and other regulatory issues. Here are a few paragraphs describing some of these considerations:

Clear Contract Terms

The company should ensure that its contract with the marketing agency includes clear terms regarding ownership of intellectual property (IP) rights, data privacy, and compliance with relevant regulations. The contract should specify who owns the IP rights to the content generated by the AI technology and how the company can use and distribute the content. Additionally, the contract should address how the agency will handle sensitive information, such as customer data, and what measures they will take to protect it.

Data Privacy and Security

The company should ensure the marketing agency has robust data privacy and security policies to protect sensitive information. The agency should have strict access controls, encryption, and other appropriate safeguards to prevent unauthorized access or misuse of customer data. The company should also conduct due diligence on the agency's data handling practices before sharing sensitive information.

Regulatory Compliance

The company should ensure that the marketing agency is compliant with relevant regulations, such as data privacy and consumer protection laws. The company should also be aware of any specific regulations that apply to their industry or products and ensure that the agency complies with these regulations.

For example, suppose the company is operating in a highly regulated industry such as healthcare or finance. In that case, they may need to require the agency to obtain specific certifications or licenses before working on their account.

Content Review and Approval

The company should establish a clear process for reviewing and approving content generated by the marketing agency's AI technology. This should include regular reviews of content to ensure that it meets the company's standards and does not violate any regulations or laws. Additionally, the company should have a clear process for rejecting or modifying content that does not meet its standards or is in violation of regulations.

Auditing and Monitoring

The company should conduct regular audits of the marketing agency's use of AI technology to ensure compliance with their contract and any relevant regulations. This may include monitoring the agency's data handling practices, reviewing its content generation processes, and ensuring it uses appropriate security measures to protect sensitive information. Additionally, the company should have a clear process for addressing any issues or concerns that arise during these audits.

Legal Compliance

The company should ensure that the marketing agency complies with all relevant legal requirements, such as copyright and consumer protection laws. This may involve reviewing the agency's content to ensure it does not infringe on existing copyrights or violate any laws. Additionally, the company should be aware of any specific legal requirements that apply to their industry or products and ensure that the agency complies with these requirements.

Transparency and Accountability

The company should require the marketing agency to provide regular reports on their use of AI technology, including information on how they generate content, what data they use, and how they protect sensitive information. This will help ensure that the company is aware of any potential issues or concerns and can address them proactively. Additionally, the company should establish clear lines of accountability within the agency so that there is a clear understanding of who is responsible for what.

In summary, companies that hire external marketing agencies to create content using generative AI technologies should take several considerations to protect themselves from potential intellectual property, data privacy, and other regulatory issues. These include establishing clear contract terms, ensuring data privacy and security, complying with relevant regulations, reviewing and approving content, auditing and monitoring the agency's use of AI technology, ensuring legal compliance, and promoting transparency and accountability within the agency. By taking these steps, companies can ensure their use of generative AI technologies is both effective and responsible.

Conclusion

The integration of generative AI in businesses can present several challenges that need to be addressed proactively. These challenges include the impact on time and quality of work, the importance of data quality, legal and regulatory issues, and what to do if the company hires external agencies and contractors that might use generative AI.

To address these challenges effectively, companies must be willing to invest in proper training and education for their employees, ensure the quality of the data used in the AI systems, and stay up-to-date with the latest legal and regulatory developments related to generative AI. Additionally, companies should carefully consider the terms of their contracts with external agencies and contractors who use generative AI on their behalf and ensure that they have the necessary resources and expertise to manage these challenges effectively.

Ultimately, the successful integration of generative AI in businesses will require careful planning, strategic decision-making, and a commitment to addressing the potential challenges proactively. By taking these steps, companies can unlock the full potential of generative AI and achieve significant benefits for their operations, customer experience, and bottom line.

3.3 Integrating Generative AI into Your Workflow

As you surely know, even if your organization is completely bought into exploring ways to incorporate generative AI into your processes and your work product, it's not that simple to do so, particularly in an enterprise environment. In this chapter, we will look at some considerations for integrating generative AI based on the four foundational components of any type of transformation:

- People
- Processes
- Data
- Platforms

Those familiar with this approach may not have been expecting the third item, data, to be in there, but I have started insisting that it be included and separated from the other three. Particularly in a world where AI plays such a key role, good data quality, access, and governance are critical.

Keep in mind also that we will primarily focus on things from a *marketing* and a *marketer's* perspective. We may touch on some other areas of the business, but if we were to talk about *all* of the areas generative AI can play a role in across all teams in a company, we might be here all day!

People

We will start with the people aspect of integrating generative AI into your workflows. Preparing your people to use generative AI effectively requires a focus on education, process changes, and cultural shifts. It is also important to note that a shift to greater usage of AI will not be without its shifts in labor. For instance, research from Staffing Industry Analytics (SIA) reflected that AI could increase the total contract and staffing industry workers on assignment by 9% over the next 3 years, while AI will replace 39% of tasks from both internal workers and staffing industry workers[26].

Here are some ways that organizations can train and ready their people for this new technology:

Roles

Has your company hired a "prompt engineer" yet? If you've followed the headlines recently, these roles can demand upwards of $400k per year (USD) and have invited some eye-rolling for sure. I'll be completely honest: my first reaction to that title was to draw an analogy to a company in 2005 hiring a "Google Searcher" to help their teams. But very quickly did I eat my words.

That said, in a work environment where getting the best possible results from generative AI is essential, it stands to reason you would want someone well-qualified to extract the best possible content from the generative AI tools you're investing so much time and effort into.

So, what exactly is a prompt engineer? A prompt engineer is a professional who specializes in designing and optimizing language prompts or input text for natural language processing (NLP) systems, such as chatbots, voice assistants, and language translation software. The primary goal of a prompt engineer is to craft high-quality prompts that elicit accurate and relevant responses from NLP systems, enabling them to perform tasks such as answering questions, providing information, or completing tasks.

If you're interested in hiring one, I've provided a sample job description in Appendix 2 for you!

Education: upskilling and reskilling

If you aren't quite ready to invest in a full-time prompt engineer position, and even if you *are*, there are many other things you should be doing as well. These include *upskilling* your current team members, where AI can augment some small portion of their roles, and reskilling team members whose jobs can be automated significantly. While this isn't a book about company culture, suffice it to say that if you have a great employee, you want to keep them, even if it involves training them in some new areas of expertise.

Organizations should provide training and education programs to help employees understand the basics of generative AI and how it works.

This can include online courses, workshops, and in-person training sessions.

This education can also include not only *how* to use generative AI but also *when* to use it and (as importantly) when *not* to use it, whether for regulatory or compliance reasons or otherwise.

Cultural shifts

The large-scale adoption of generative AI and other AI tools in a company can significantly impact the organization's culture. Here are some potential effects:

- **Changes in job responsibilities:** As AI tools take over more routine and repetitive tasks, employees may need to adapt their roles to focus on higher-value tasks such as strategy, creativity, and problem-solving. This can be a challenging transition for some employees, especially if they have been doing the same tasks for a long time.

- **Shift in skill sets:** As AI becomes more prevalent, employees may need to develop new skills to work effectively with these tools. For example, marketers may need to learn to use AI-powered tools for data analysis, content creation, and campaign optimization.

- **New roles and opportunities:** On the other hand, adopting AI can also create new roles and opportunities within the company. For example, a company may need to hire AI engineers, data scientists, or machine learning specialists to develop and maintain their AI systems.

- **Changes in communication:** As AI tools become more prevalent, communication within the company may change. For example, employees may need to adapt to using chatbots or virtual assistants for routine tasks rather than communicating directly with human colleagues.
- **Potential for bias:** There is also the potential for bias in AI systems, which can have cultural implications. For example, if an AI system is biased against certain groups of people, this could lead to unfair treatment or discrimination.

All of this change related to AI adoption means that leaders need to account for the anxiety, confusion, and potential disengagement that can happen during this or any other transition. To ensure that team members stay engaged through this transition, a marketing leader could take the following positive steps:

- Communicate clearly and regularly: It's essential to communicate with employees about the changes happening and why they are necessary. This can help to build trust and understanding.
- Provide training and development opportunities: Offer training and development opportunities to help employees develop new skills and adapt to the changing role of their work.

- Encourage collaboration: Encourage collaboration between humans and AI systems to ensure employees understand how to use these tools effectively.
- Foster a culture of creativity and innovation: Encourage employees to think creatively about using AI tools to enhance their work and create new opportunities.
- Monitor for bias: Be aware of the potential for bias in AI systems and take steps to mitigate this, such as using diverse data sets and testing for bias before deployment.
- Celebrate successes: Celebrate the successes of employees adapting well to the changes brought about by AI adoption. This can help to build morale and motivation.
- Be open to feedback: Encourage employees to provide feedback on the impact of AI on their work and listen to their concerns. This can help to identify potential issues early and address them before they become major problems.

Overall, the adoption of generative AI and other AI tools in a company can have significant cultural implications. By being proactive in communicating with employees, providing training and development opportunities, encouraging collaboration, fostering a culture of creativity and innovation, monitoring for bias, celebrating successes, and being open to feedback, marketing leaders can help their teams stay engaged through this transition and thrive in the new AI-driven work environment.

Process

To better incorporate generative AI into their workflow, organizations should consider changing or modifying their processes in several key areas. Keep in mind that some of these areas have been touched on briefly as we discussed other areas in previous chapters, so I'm not going to belabor some of these points.

Here are some ways that organizations can modify their processes to make the most of generative AI:

- **Idea generation:** Generative AI can be used to generate new ideas and approaches to problems. Organizations should modify their processes to include generative AI as a tool for idea generation, allowing it to provide additional variations of ideas and approaches.

- **Prototype development:** Generative AI can also be used to develop prototypes of new products or designs quickly. Organizations should modify their processes to include generative AI as a tool for prototype development, allowing it to generate and test multiple variations of designs quickly.

- **Decision-making:** Generative AI can be used to analyze large amounts of data and provide insights that can inform decision-making. Organizations should modify their processes to include generative AI as a tool for decision-making, allowing it to provide additional insights and analysis.

- **Collaboration:** Generative AI can be used to facilitate collaboration between team members, allowing them to work together more effectively. Organizations should modify their processes to include generative AI as a tool for collaboration, allowing it to facilitate communication and idea-sharing.

- **Transparency:** Create processes and be transparent about when AI can be used and when it should not be used. You should be realistic about the fact that teams are likely going to be using these tools already, had used them at a previous job or contract, and many have already adopted methods to make their work incredibly efficient using them. Instead of making their use a bad thing, embrace it with some guardrails in place.

- **Compliance and Regulatory considerations:** Be aware of regulations and compliance that span many areas, which include consumer data privacy (such as the EU's GDPR), bias in machine learning, industry-specific regulations that relate to customer data (such as HIPAA for healthcare), or others, whether those are imposed by external organizations or any ethical considerations enforced internally. For more details here, we discussed this in greater depth in the previous chapter under "Legal and Regulatory" things to watch out for.

While we briefly covered these process aspects, don't think there isn't quite a bit to unpack once you start doing so. In fact, you might want to consider incorporating AI-specific guidance and governance into your marketing operations or project management office (PMO) to ensure consistency and transparency and that there are continuous improvement systems in place in this fast-moving space.

Data

While some data considerations may overlap with the next section, platforms, as I mentioned at the beginning of this chapter, I think it's important to keep them separate to ensure enough attention gets placed on each. As generative AI becomes more prevalent in marketing, marketing leaders need to pay attention to and take the following steps to prepare for its greater adoption, specifically when it comes to data:

- **Assess current data infrastructure:** Review the current data infrastructure to ensure it can handle the volume, variety, and velocity of data generated by AI systems. This includes data storage, processing power, and network bandwidth.
- **Develop a data governance strategy:** Establish a data governance strategy that ensures data quality, security, and compliance with regulations such as GDPR and CCPA. This should include policies for data access, sharing, and deletion.

- **Define data privacy and security protocols:** Develop protocols to protect customer data and ensure it is not used in ways that could be harmful or exploitative. This includes implementing encryption, access controls, and auditing mechanisms.

- **Prepare for the ethical implications of AI-generated data:** Consider the potential ethical implications of using AI-generated data, such as the potential for bias or discrimination. Develop guidelines for ethical use of AI-generated data and ensure employees are trained on these protocols.

- **Develop a plan for managing and integrating AI-generated data:** Determine how AI-generated data will be integrated into existing systems and processes, such as customer relationship management (CRM) software or marketing automation platforms.

- **Invest in AI-powered data analytics tools:** Consider investing in AI-powered data analytics tools to gain insights from large datasets and make more accurate predictions about customer behavior.

- **Monitor and analyze AI-generated data:** Regularly monitor and analyze the data generated by AI systems to ensure that it is accurate, relevant, and unbiased. This includes testing and evaluating AI models for potential biases or errors.

- **Develop a plan for handling and responding to AI-related incidents:** Establish a plan for handling and responding to AI-related incidents such as data breaches, algorithmic bias, or system failures.

- **Consider the impact of AI on customer trust:** As AI becomes more prevalent in marketing, consider the potential impact on customer trust. Ensure that customers know how their data is being used and that they have control over their personal information.

- **Stay up-to-date with regulations and industry standards:** Keep up to date with evolving regulations and industry standards related to AI and data privacy, such as the European Union's General Data Protection Regulation (GDPR) and the California Consumer Privacy Act (CCPA).

Taking these steps, marketing leaders can help ensure that their organizations are prepared for the greater adoption of generative AI in marketing and can effectively manage the data generated by these systems.

Platforms

In this book, we've already talked about platforms in a few different ways, so I want to avoid redundancy here. We won't rehash the types of generative AI applications (you can see that in Part 2 of this book). Instead, let's look at a few things to consider when selecting generative AI platforms to incorporate.

When deciding whether to adopt a specific generative AI tool, a marketing team should consider several factors to ensure a successful implementation. These considerations include:

- **How it fits into their current workflow:** The team should assess how the new tool aligns with their current marketing workflow and processes. Will it replace existing tools or augment them? How will it impact the team's workload and productivity? A poor fit can lead to resistance, low adoption rates, and wasted resources.

- **Strength of its individual features:** The team should evaluate the tool's features and capabilities, considering their specific needs and goals. Does the tool offer the necessary functionality to support their marketing strategies? Are there any gaps in features that may hinder its effectiveness?

- **Existing platform capabilities:** The team should consider if an existing platform could perform most of the tasks of the new tool, potentially saving the company money. They should weigh the benefits of integrating a new tool against the cost and potential disruption to their current workflow.

- **New processes needed for integration:** The team should assess what new processes may be needed to integrate the tool into their workflow. This includes training, data integration, and ongoing maintenance requirements. They should consider the resource implications of implementing and maintaining the tool.

- **Potential risks:** In highly regulated environments or where consumer data privacy is a top concern, the team should carefully evaluate potential risks associated with the new tool. These may include security breaches, data privacy violations, or unintended consequences. They should ensure the tool complies with relevant regulations and industry standards, such as GDPR and CCPA.

- **Vendor support and service:** The team should evaluate the vendor's support and service capabilities, including documentation, training, and technical assistance. A reliable and responsive vendor can make a significant difference in the tool's success.

- **Scalability:** The team should consider if the tool is scalable enough to accommodate their future growth and changing needs. Will it be able to handle increased volume or new marketing channels?

- **Integration with other tools:** The team should assess how well the tool integrates with their existing marketing tools and systems, such as CRM, marketing automation, or analytics platforms. Seamless integration can improve efficiency and productivity.

- **Customization options:** The team should evaluate whether the tool offers sufficient customization options to fit their specific needs and branding requirements. Can they tailor the tool to meet their unique goals and objectives?

- **Long-term commitment:** Finally, the team should consider their long-term commitment to the tool and the potential for future updates and enhancements. Will the vendor continue to invest in the tool's development and innovation?

By carefully considering these factors, a marketing team can make an informed decision about adopting a specific generative AI tool and ensure its successful integration into their workflow, maximizing its benefits and minimizing potential risks.

Conclusion

Incorporating generative AI into a company's marketing efforts can profoundly impact the people, processes, data, and platforms used within the organization. By leveraging these powerful tools, marketers can streamline their workflows, gain valuable insights from data, and create more personalized and engaging customer experiences.

However, to successfully integrate generative AI into their marketing efforts, marketers must be mindful of these technologies' potential risks and challenges, such as data privacy concerns and the need for ongoing training and maintenance.

3.4 Doing Generative AI Well

As we've discussed already, and you're surely seeing on a daily basis, it is hard to escape the hype around generative AI. That said, using generative AI well takes more than simply typing in a prompt and hoping for the best. It takes a solid approach, coordination across your existing processes and teams, and the right platforms for the job.

When I talked with Jonathan Boakes, Managing Director of Infinum, he offered the following:

> *"There is no one-size-fits-all approach to AI adoption and businesses should tailor their AI strategy to specific needs and objectives, whether this is in-house or user facing. Some businesses may lean toward innovation, while others may tread more cautiously, implementing once risks and opportunities are clearer.*
>
> *In industries like oil and gas, Generative AI is playing a crucial role through processing and analysing vast datasets. This includes analysing sequences and simulations to identify potential risks and improve safety protocols. AI's ability to collate and comprehend mass datasets efficiently is significantly impactful."*

In other words, there are a lot of opportunities, across a lot of industries, but those opportunities vary widely by organizational maturity, industry maturity and regulations, and many other factors that require a deliberate approach.

After discussing several aspects of generative AI over the course of this book, let's talk about using AI effectively and the factors to consider when adopting generative AI so that you and your teams can go beyond simply jumping on the bandwagon and instead become power users.

Set the ground rules first

You would think that from all the hype there is about the benefits of generative AI, it must be a good fit in every situation. But of course, as with anything, there needs to be a solid understanding of its benefits and drawbacks so that teams can utilize it effectively and avoid unintended risks.

Thus, it's essential to establish clear ground rules for its use. This includes defining the specific goals and objectives of the campaign, identifying the target audience and their preferences, and determining how the technology will be used to support those objectives. Marketers should also consider the potential risks and challenges associated with generative AI, such as the risk of bias in the training data or the potential for over-personalization, and develop strategies to mitigate these risks. Additionally, it's important for marketers to establish clear guidelines on when generative AI should *not* be used or where there are legal, ethical, or other regulatory concerns about its usage.

By setting these ground rules and understanding the limitations of generative AI, marketers can ensure that they are using the technology effectively and responsibly to achieve their goals.

Use it at the right time in your workflow

Generative AI is most effective when integrated into the workflow at the right time. For example, marketers can use generative AI at the beginning of the process to help develop initial concepts or ideas or early on to help refine and iterate on existing drafts. By leveraging generative AI at these stages, marketers can create a wider range of options and explore more innovative and effective campaign ideas. Additionally, generative AI can be used later on in the process to create multiple variations of content once a concept and campaign idea has been finalized.

By incorporating generative AI into the workflow at the right time, marketers can streamline their creative process, reduce the time and effort required to develop high-quality content, and increase the likelihood of success.

Find the right tool for the job

While, as we've seen, generative AI can be a powerful tool for marketing teams of all types and sizes, it's essential to find the right tools for the job rather than simply relying on what may be easy to access or readily available.

Numerous generative AI platforms are available, each with its own strengths and weaknesses depending on the specific use case. For example, some platforms may be better suited for specific types of content generation, like social media posts, while others may be more effective for image generation or other purposes like video, design layouts, and more. To get the best results, marketers need to take the time to evaluate potential generative AI platforms and choose the one that is best aligned with their campaign goals and target audience.

It is also important to note that legacy applications and platforms are now rapidly adopting generative AI features, so you may want to take a second look at tools you already use for new features that won't require you to adopt a brand-new platform.

Get better at writing prompts

If you want to up your generative AI game, you and your team need to be great at writing prompts. A well-crafted prompt guides the generation of high-quality, relevant, and engaging content that resonates more effectively with the target audience. By providing clear and specific direction, marketers can help the generative AI platform understand what they are looking for and produce content that meets their needs. Strong prompts can also help to mitigate the risk of bias in the generated content and ensure that the final product is consistent with the desired tone and style.

As an example, think about your early experience with search engines—mine dates back to the 90s when tools like Lycos, AltaVista, and others predated Google. While you may not have thought about it at the time, your first queries (as well as the quality of the search engine algorithms) were not nearly as nuanced and sophisticated as the ones that you perform today, and when and how you use search in your daily life has likely evolved as well. The same goes for prompt writing.

So, take the time to learn what makes a good prompt and experiment with different approaches. Ensure to share your learnings as a team as well, so all can benefit. Some team members may be naturals at this (as some people seem to be better at conducting search engine queries than others), so find ways to teach and train on creating prompts because this is a skill all can benefit from.

Make sure it augments but doesn't replace the human aspect

Finally, let's not forget our humanity in the race to utilize the latest artificial intelligence. While generative AI can be an amazing tool, there are good times to use it and less useful ones. Don't think of generative AI as a replacement for people but as an augmentation of their abilities.

Therefore, generative AI can work really well as a starting point, an idea generator, or a way to generate multiple ideas based on something existing. This means that the human teams working with it can lend their strategy, creativity, and common sense to ensure that AI-generated content makes sense and will help achieve the desired results.

Conclusion

Upping your generative AI game involves being thoughtful at many points in the process. Understanding how important this set of tools can be is not enough. You need to ensure your teams are knowledgeable, using the right tools and having some guidance on when and where they can use generative AI to be most effective.

Conclusion

I hope you've found this guide valuable in your quest to learn more about and embrace generative AI! If you didn't know already before you started reading this book, it should now be clear to you that this is a very fast-moving field, with new product offerings, features, and legal/regulatory implications popping up daily. Thus, it's important to know the fundamentals and ensure you are regularly keeping up to date with the movement happening around us in this space.

Jonathan Boakes from Infinum offers some great advice here:

> *"Jumping into AI without a solid plan can lead to costly failures for everyone involved. So, careful planning and learning from past experiences are essential for success in this AI-driven age.*
>
> *It's advisable to begin with small-scale pilots, creating a simulation environment to gain a deeper understanding of Generative AI without risking large investments.*
>
> *The most significant area of caution when adopting Generative AI is data security and potential biases. Organisations must prioritise data governance and guard against exposing sensitive customer data.*

Unprotected data harvesting can feed AI bias and misconduct and when the result isn't right, it is based on existing data sources we can't entirely verify. It's a quagmire that must be safely navigated. Generative AI holds significant promise, but its adoption should be purpose-driven, cautious, and ethical. Organisations can harness its potential by strategically planning, starting small, and ensuring data security and ethics are at the forefront of their AI initiatives."

Let's recap some of the things we've discussed over the previous pages and talk a little more specifically about optimization and continuous improvement. Specifically, we'll delve into the governance of AI utilization, ensuring there is continuing innovation in AI usage, and how to think about effective measurement of your AI usage.

Governance of AI Utilization

Governance is all about ensuring that your company's AI usage aligns with the organization's goals and values. This means your AI systems should be transparent, ethical, and secure. To achieve this, you should have a clear code of conduct that governs how your AI systems operate, set up data usage and sharing standards among team members, and put processes and procedures in place to ensure that AI solutions are vetted and evaluated regularly. Doing so will ensure that your systems are effective, safe, and transparent.

Ensuring There is Continuing Innovation in AI Usage

Innovation is a key driver of success in any industry, and it's no different when it comes to AI utilization. To get the most out of your AI systems, you need to stay updated with the latest developments in AI technology. This means you need to invest in ongoing training for your team members, keep an eye on emerging technologies and trends, and foster a culture of experimentation and risk-taking within your organization. By cultivating a strong innovation ecosystem, you can help ensure that your AI solutions are always cutting edge and ahead of the curve.

Effective Measurement of AI Usage

As with any other business initiative, measuring the effectiveness of your AI systems is crucial. You need to clearly understand the metrics that matter most to your organization, such as ROI, customer satisfaction, and employee engagement. You should also set up a system for tracking and analyzing these metrics regularly and use this information to fine-tune your systems and investments regularly. Doing so will ensure that your AI usage aligns with your organization's goals and helps you achieve success over time.

Training and Up-Skilling Your Team Members

As discussed in the previous section on integrating generative AI into your teams and processes, investing in ongoing training and up-skilling for your team members is important. AI is a complex field; even the most seasoned veterans can benefit from ongoing education and training opportunities. By making training a part of your organizational culture, you can help up-skill your team members, increase their engagement and retention, and ensure that your AI deployment is always successful.

Staying up to date on the latest tools, platforms, and technologies

It might go without saying, but in addition to training and up-skilling, you will want to ensure that you are continually evaluating new tools and platforms, as this is an incredibly fast-moving space. Things may cool down in the months and years ahead, but for now, there are countless potential tools, often with different focus areas.

Another thing to remember is that many legacy platforms are also quickly adopting generative AI components. This means everything from Adobe Photoshop to Hubspot and Salesforce to Microsoft Office are making generative AI a part of the software tools you and your team already rely on. This means you don't always have to *switch from* an existing platform to get the benefits of a generative approach, but it does mean that you should have a stance on when and how to use some of these features. The same governance rules apply whether it's a startup platform with ten employees or whether it is software from a multi-billion dollar established organization.

Generative AI holds great promise for marketing and other business functions, but it's important to use it effectively. By following the best practices outlined in this article – governance of AI utilization, ensuring there is continuing innovation in AI usage, effective measurement of your AI usage, and investing in training and up-skilling your team members – you can help ensure that your AI systems are cutting edge, transparent, effective, and aligned with your organization's goals and values. So why not start applying these principles to your organization today? The results could be transformative.

Thanks again for joining me in another Agile Brand Guide, and I wish you the best in your generative AI adoption and all the great content and experiences you create!

About the Author

Greg Kihlström is a best-selling author, speaker, and entrepreneur, currently an advisor and consultant to top companies on marketing technology, customer experience, and digital transformation initiatives. He is also the host of The Agile Brand with Greg Kihlström podcast. He is a two-time CEO and Co-Founder, growing both companies organically and through acquisitions and ultimately leading both to be acquired (one in 2017 and the other in 2021). He has worked with some of the world's top brands, including Adidas, Choice Hotels, Coca-Cola, Dell, FedEx, HP, Marriott, MTV, Starbucks, Toyota, and VMware.

He earned his MBA from Quantic School of Business and Technology and is a member of the School of Marketing Faculty at the Association of National Advertisers. He currently serves on the University of Richmond's Customer Experience Advisory Board and the Workhouse Arts Foundation Board as Chair of the Marketing Committee. Greg was the founding Chair of the American Advertising Federation's National Innovation Committee and served on the Virginia Tech Pamplin College of Business Marketing Mentorship Advisory Board. Greg is Lean Six Sigma Black Belt certified, is an Agile Certified Coach (ICP-ACC) and holds a certification in Business Agility (ICP-BAF).

Greg has had multiple internationally best-selling books, including his Agile Brand Guides series on marketing technology platforms and practices. His eleventh and most recent book, *House of the Customer*

(2023), discusses the 1:1 personalized customer experience of the future and how brands can organize the people, processes, and platforms that enable it. *Meaningful Measurement of the Customer Experience* (2022) provides guidance on creating a customer-centric culture that prioritizes customer needs while aligning internal teams around a common goal. His award-winning podcast, "The Agile Brand with Greg Kihlström", launched in early 2019, discusses brand strategy, marketing, and customer experience with some of the world's leading experts and leaders.

Greg is a contributing writer to Fast Company, Forbes, MarTech, and CMSWire and has been featured in publications such as Advertising Age and The Washington Post. Greg has been named a 2022 Top 10 Marketing and Customer Experience Thought Leader by Thinkers 360, was named one of ICMI's Top 25 CX Thought Leaders two years in a row, and a DC Inno 50 on Fire as a DC trendsetter in Marketing. He's participated as a keynote speaker and panelist at industry events worldwide, including Internet Week New York, Internet Summit, DigiMarCon, Digital Summit, EventTech, MarTech, SMX Social Media, and VMworld. He has guest lectured at several colleges and universities, including VCU Brandcenter, Georgetown University, Duke University, American University, University of Maryland, Howard University, and Virginia Tech.

Greg lives in Alexandria, Virginia, with his wife, Lindsey.

Appendix 1: Martechipedia Generative AI Listings

The following listings come from The Agile Brand Guide's Martechipedia listing of Generative AI platforms. This is not an exhaustive list, but we maintain a list of some of the most popular platforms here, and the list is constantly growing.

If you represent a generative AI platform and want to update your listing (or add one) or are a generative AI user and wish to contribute to your favorite platform, you can visit the website to do so. For more information about the platforms, go to https://agilebrandguide.com/directory/directory_category/generative-ai/, or you can go directly to the platform websites. Most have some type of free trial or ability to sign up, though these vary by the platform.

Now, let's look at some examples of seven categories of generative AI platforms:

- Audio Generation
- Design Generation
- Image Generation
- Marketing tools
- Music Generation
- Text Generation
- Video Generation

Please keep in mind that this is a fast-moving space, so the information here is likely to change over time. We do our best to keep the online listing up to date, but also rely on site visitors and platform owners to update their listings.

Audio Generation

Murf
Creates voice overs for different contexts; enables adding punctuation, and provides the commercial rights of the content

Parent Company: Murf

https://murf.ai/

Play.ht
Provides AI-generated voices useful for various commercial purposes, offers services in more than 140 languages, and enables text-to-speech conversion.

Parent Company: Play.ht

https://play.ht/

Replica

Enables text-to-speech conversion, and offers AI-generated voices.

Parent Company: Replica

https://www.replicastudios.com/

Speechify

Allows text-to-speech conversion while enabling the adjustment of reading speed and offering realistic AI-generated voices

Parent Company: Speechify

https://speechify.com/

Design Generation

Colormind

Allows creating color palettes based on a movie scene, artwork, or other images using Generative AI.

Parent Company: Colormind

http://colormind.io/

Designs.ai

Allows generating logos and banners, provides design templates; and enables the export of the produced items to different formats.

Parent Company: Designs.ai

https://designs.ai/

Fronty AI

Allows creating websites compatible with mobile devices and SEO necessities.

Parent Company: Fronty AI

https://fronty.com/

Khroma

Khroma uses Generative AI to learn which colors you like and creates palettes based on your preferences.

Parent Company: khroma

https://www.khroma.co/

Uizard

Uizard generates designs for UI including mobile apps; websites and more.

Parent Company: Uizard Technologies

https://uizard.io/

Image Generation

Adobe Firefly

Currently in Beta (as of the writing of this guide) from Adobe. Allows several functions using generative AI including text to image, generative fill, text effects, generative recolor, 3D to image and extend image.

Parent Company: Adobe

https://www.adobe.com/sensei/generative-ai/firefly.html

Artbreeder

Creates AI-generated collages; and generates images with the option of manipulating the age; gender; and other characteristics of the subject.

Parent Company: Morphogen

https://www.artbreeder.com/

Craiyon

Converts text-to-image; not suitable for the creation of larger images

Parent Company: Craiyon

https://www.craiyon.com/

DALL-E

From the website: DALL·E 2 is an AI system that can create realistic images and art from a description in natural language.

Parent Company: OpenAI

https://openai.com/dall-e-2

Draw3D

Uses Generative AI to turn sketches into 3D photorealistic images

Parent Company: Kites.Dev

https://draw3d.online/

Lensa

Lensa uses generative AI for photo retouching and includes a mobile app.

Parent Company: Prisma Labs

https://prisma-ai.com/lensa

Midjourney

Midjourney is a generative artificial intelligence program and service created and hosted by San Francisco-based independent research lab Midjourney, Inc.

Parent Company: Midjourney Inc.

https://www.midjourney.com/

NightCafe

Art generation with different styles and resolution options

Parent Company: NightCafe

https://creator.nightcafe.studio/

Shutterstock AI Image Generator

Generative AI that generates images from a text prompt from the stock photo platform Shutterstock.

Parent Company: Shutterstock

https://www.shutterstock.com/ai-image-generator

Stable Diffusion

Stable Diffusion is a deep learning, text-to-image model released in 2022 based on diffusion techniques. It is primarily used to generate detailed images conditioned on text descriptions, though it can also be applied to …

Parent Company: Stability AI

https://stability.ai/

starryai

Uses Generative AI to create art through text prompts with a focus on artistic illustrations.

Parent Company: starryai

https://starryai.com/

Marketing Tools

AdCreative.ai

Creates designs and multiple types of marketing creatives using Generative AI.

Parent Company: Adcreative.ai

https://www.adcreative.ai/

Tailwind

Tailwind has several components available for marketers including generative AI for marketing content creation, marketing plan creation, and social media scheduling.

Parent Company: Tailwind

https://www.tailwindapp.com/

tinyEinstein

An AI marketing manager that helps brands optimize their Shopify stores.

Parent Company: tinyEinstein

https://www.tinyeinstein.ai/

Music Generation

AIVA

Generative AI that composes music for movies, commercials, games and tv shows.

Parent Company: AIVA Technologies

http://www.aiva.ai

Descript Overdub

Descript's Overdub lets you create a text-to-speech model of your voice or select one from our ultra-realistic stock voices.

Parent Company: Descript

https://www.descript.com/overdub

Text Generation

AdCreative.ai

Creates designs and multiple types of marketing creatives using Generative AI.

Parent Company: Adcreative.ai

https://www.adcreative.ai/

Anyword

Anyword is generative AI platform that allows marketers to create scalable, on-brand content that converts and drives sales.

Parent Company: Keywee, Inc.

https://anyword.com/

Bard

Bard, considered Google's response to ChatGPT, is a chatbot and content generation tool that runs on LaMDA, a transformer-based model that Google launched a couple of years ago. The tool …

Parent Company: Google/Alphabet

https://bard.google.com/

ChatGPT

ChatGPT is OpenAI's most popular tool to date, giving the everyday user free access to basic AI content generation. For users who require more processing power, early access to new features …

Parent Company: OpenAI

https://chat.openai.com/auth/login

Cohere Generate

Cohere Generate is a text generation solution from Cohere, a startup with leadership members who contributed to Google's Transformer paper.

Parent Company: Cohere

https://cohere.com/generate

Frase IO

Produces slogans, product summaries, introductions, articles and blogs, titles and product descriptions.

Parent Company: Frase IO

https://www.frase.io/

Jasper

Generative AI for on-brand marketing content in a variety of formats. Jasper is targeted primarily at marketers and can create content in a variety of formats and for a wide variety of target channels.

https://www.jasper.ai

Peppertype

Offers ready-made templates for creating meta descriptions, articles and blog posts, and emails; enables commercial use of the content that is produced.

Parent Company: Peppertype

https://www.peppercontent.io/product/content-marketing-platform/

Rytr

Generative AI platform that provides text-based content for a variety of formats, from blogs to emails, to ad copy. It is flexible in the style and tone and easy to use.

Parent Company: Rytr

https://rytr.me

Swell AI

Automate writing articles and shownotes for podcasts and videos. Upload & repurpose your audio and video content at scale.

Parent Company: Swell AI

https://swellai.com/

Tailwind

Tailwind has several components available for marketers including generative AI for marketing content creation, marketing plan creation, and social media scheduling.

Parent Company: Tailwind

https://www.tailwindapp.com/

tinyEinstein

An AI marketing manager that helps brands optimize their Shopify stores..

Parent Company: tinyEinstein

https://www.tinyeinstein.ai/

Writer

Writer is a generative AI platform that can incorporate a company's own data, style, and brand guidelines, and has enterprise-grade security and data privacy features.

Parent Company: Writer

https://www.writer.com

Writesonic

Writesonic makes it super easy and fast for you to compose high-performing landing pages, product descriptions, ads, and blog posts in seconds.

Parent Company: Writesonic, Inc.

https://www.writesonic.com

Video Generation

Deepshot

Deepshot is the world's first fully customizable dialogue generation and replacement software; allowing you to create professional-looking videos with ease. Generate content quickly with intuitive user profiles.

Parent Company: Deepshot

https://www.deepshot.ai/

Elai

Allows for the conversion of a blog post or an article to a video; offers more than 25 avatars; and produces personalized avatars for customers.

Parent Company: Elai

https://elai.io/

Flexclip

Supports Generative AI video creation; offers video editing tools; such as adding transitions; filters, or removing backgrounds

Parent Company: PearlMountain

https://www.flexclip.com/

Gan.AI

Uses Generative AI to generate hyper-customized videos using studio-quality AI video personalization tools.

Parent Company: Gan.AI

https://gan.ai/

Lumen5

Offers templates to create original videos based on presentations; or online meeting recordings

Parent Company: Lumen5

https://lumen5.com/

Oxolo

Oxolo uses Generative AI to create product videos for e-commerce.

Parent Company: Oxolo

https://www.oxolo.com/

Peech

Generative AI for video allows marketing and training teams to create branded video content from their available assets and provided in a number of formats, subtitles, and other localization features.

Parent Company: Peech

https://www.peech-ai.com/

Runway Gen-2

Runway Gen-2 allows the creation of videos using text prompts and includes the ability to edit, adjust, and collaborate in real-time in the cloud.

Parent Company: Runway AI

https://runwayml.com/ai-magic-tools/gen-2/

Synthesia

AI video creation platform that allows users to create videos based on their own scripted prompts. From there, the tool is able to use its library of AI avatars, voices and more.

Parent Company: Synthesia

https://www.synthesia.io/

Veed.io

Video generation and editing; adding subtitles; removing background noises; and resizing the videos

Parent Company: Veed.io

https://www.veed.io/

Appendix 2: Prompt Engineer Job Description

Job Title:

Prompt Engineer

Company: [Company Name]

Location: [Location]

Job Type: Full-time

About Us:

I will leave this to you!

Job Summary:

As a prompt engineer at [Company Name], you will be responsible for designing and optimizing language prompts that drive accurate and relevant responses from our generative AI and natural language processing (NLP) systems. You will work closely with other teams within the organization (e.g., marketing, communications, and others) to ensure that our prompts are of the highest quality and ensure the best outcomes from prompt-based work throughout the organization.

Key Responsibilities:

- Design and optimize language prompts for our AI-based systems, including generative AI tools, chatbots, voice assistants, and language translation software.

- Collaborate with cross-functional teams, including product development, data science, and software engineering, to ensure prompt quality and accuracy.

- Develop and maintain a comprehensive library of prompts that can be used across teams utilizing multiple NLP applications.

- Conduct A/B testing and experimentation to improve prompt performance and accuracy continually.

- Analyze and interpret data to identify trends, patterns, and areas for improvement in prompt design and optimization.

- Stay up-to-date with the latest advancements in NLP and language processing technology, and apply this knowledge to improve prompt design and optimization techniques.

Requirements:

- (College degrees may be optional, of course, but if they are required) Bachelor's degree in Computer Science, Linguistics, Marketing, Communications, or a related field

- Strong writing skills, including critical thinking and writing, and a strong understanding of language structures, syntax, and semantics

- 3+ years of experience in NLP, natural language understanding, or a related field
- Proven track record of developing high-quality prompts that elicit accurate and relevant responses from generative AI and other NLP-based systems
- Familiarity with machine learning and deep learning algorithms, particularly in the context of NLP
- Excellent problem-solving skills and ability to work independently or as part of a team
- Strong communication and collaboration skills

Nice to Have:

- Master's degree in Computer Science, Linguistics, or a related field.
- Experience with popular NLP frameworks and libraries, such as TensorFlow, PyTorch, or spaCy.
- Familiarity with cloud-based platforms and infrastructure, such as AWS or GCP.
- Knowledge of software development methodologies, including Agile and Scrum.

Resources and References

Many great resources that can complement the ideas in this book are available for marketing technology professionals. Below are a few related to The Agile Brand and Greg Kihlström's other work.

For other resources outside of those below, you can reach out to Greg Kihlström over LinkedIn, and he can likely point you in the right direction!

https://www.linkedin.com/in/gregkihlstrom/

Resources

The Agile Brand Guide website provides articles, product information, and Martechipedia, a wiki full of marketing, technology, and AI terms. You can find more information here: https://agilebrandguide.com/

The Agile Brand with Greg Kihlström podcast features interviews with marketing and technology leaders from top brands and platforms, with many conversations centering on generative AI and other applications of artificial intelligence. You can find more information here:

https://www.gregkihlstrom.com/theagilebrandpodcast

References

[1] Reuters. (2023, February 1). ChatGPT sets record for fastest growing user base: Analyst note. Retrieved from <https://www.reuters.com/technology/chatgpt-sets-record-fastest-growing-user-base-analyst-note-2023-02-01>

[2] SimplyWise. (2023). 2023 Small Business Confidence Survey. Retrieved from <https://www.simplywise.com/blog/simplywise-2023-small-business-confidence-survey/>

[3] Staffing Industry Analysts (2022, December 14). AI could bring 9% increase in workers on assignment: Collaboration in Gig Economy gets rolling. Retrieved from <https://www2.staffingindustry.com/Editorial/Daily-News/AI-could-bring-9-increase-in-workers-on-assignment-Collaboration-in-Gig-Economy-gets-rolling-66878>

[4] Infinum. "Research on Generative AI." Retrieved from <https://www.infinum.com>

[5] IEEE Spectrum (n.d.). The short, strange life of the first friendly robot. Retrieved from <https://spectrum.ieee.org/the-short-strange-life-of-the-first-friendly-robot#toggle-gdpr>

[6] Oxford University Press (2022). The effects of chatbots on mental health. Mind, 125(236), 433-986238. Retrieved from <https://academic.oup.com/mind/article/LIX/236/433/986238>

[7] Computer History Museum (n.d.). Samuel. Retrieved from <https://history.computer.org/pioneers/samuel.html>

[8] Stanford University (n.d.). Samuel. Retrieved from <http://infolab.stanford.edu/pub/voy/museum/samuel.html>

[9] Stanford University (n.d.). A History of Neural Networks. Retrieved from <https://cs.stanford.edu/people/eroberts/courses/soco/projects/neural-networks/History/history1.html>

[10] Towards Data Science (n.d.). A Concise History of Neural Networks. Retrieved from <https://towardsdatascience.com/a-concise-history-of-neural-networks-2070655d3fec>

[11] Data Versity (n.d.). A Brief History of Deep Learning. Retrieved from <https://www.dataversity.net/brief-history-deep-learning/>

[12] ING April 6, 2016. Rembrandt goes digital. Retrieved from <https://www.ing.com/Newsroom/News/Rembrandt-goes-digital-.htm>

[13] Gartner (n.d.). Generative AI. Retrieved from <https://www.gartner.com/en/topics/generative-ai>

[14] Gartner. (n.d.). Gartner Hype Cycle. Retrieved from <https://www.gartner.com/en/research/methodologies/gartner-hype-cycle>

[15] McKinsey & Company. (2022, January). The economic potential of generative AI: The next productivity frontier. Retrieved from <https://www.mckinsey.com/capabilities/mckinsey-digital/our-insights/the-economic-potential-of-generative-AI-the-next-productivity-frontier#/>

[16] Gartner (n.d.). Generative AI. Retrieved from <https://www.gartner.com/en/topics/generative-ai>

[17] McKinsey & Company. (2022, January). The economic potential of generative AI: The next productivity frontier. Retrieved from <https://www.mckinsey.com/capabilities/mckinsey-digital/our-insights/the-economic-potential-of-generative-AI-the-next-productivity-frontier#/>

[18] McKinsey & Company. (2022, January). The economic potential of generative AI: The next productivity frontier. Retrieved from

<https://www.mckinsey.com/capabilities/mckinsey-digital/our-insights/the-economic-potential-of-generative-AI-the-next-productivity-frontier#/>

[19] McKinsey & Company. (2022, April). Gen AI in high gear: Mercedes-Benz leverages the power of ChatGPT. Retrieved from <https://www.mckinsey.com/features/mckinsey-center-for-future-mobility/our-insights/drivers-of-disruption/gen-ai-in-high-gear-mercedes-benz-leverages-the-power-of-chatgpt>

[20] Society for Human Resource Management (SHRM). (2022, March). Evolving executive DEI: Diversity in the C-suite. Retrieved from <https://www.shrm.org/executive/resources/articles/pages/evolving-executive-dei-diversity-c-suite.aspx>

[21] Local Government Association (LGA). (n.d.). General Data Protection Regulation (GDPR). Retrieved from <https://www.local.gov.uk/our-support/research-and-data/data-and-transparency/general-data-protection-regulation-gdpr>

[22] European Parliament. (2023, June 1). EU AI Act: First regulation on artificial intelligence. Retrieved from <https://www.europarl.europa.eu/news/en/headlines/society/20230601STO93804/eu-ai-act-first-regulation-on-artificial-intelligence>

[23] Government of Canada, Innovation, Science and Economic Development (ISED). (n.d.). Artificial Intelligence and Data Act (AIDA) Companion Document. Retrieved from <https://ised-isde.canada.ca/site/innovation-better-canada/en/artificial-intelligence-and-data-act-aida-companion-document>

[24] The White House. (n.d.). Artificial Intelligence Bill of Rights. Retrieved from <https://www.whitehouse.gov/ostp/ai-bill-of-rights/>

[25] South China Morning Post. (2023, March 14). China sets out new rules for

generative AI in Beijing, emphasising healthy content and adherence to socialist values. Retrieved from <https://www.scmp.com/tech/big-tech/article/3227576/china-sets-out-new-rules-generative-ai-beijing-emphasising-healthy-content-and-adherence-socialist>

[26] Staffing Industry. (2023, March 15). AI could bring 9% increase in workers on assignment: Collaboration in gig economy gets rolling. Retrieved from <https://www2.staffingindustry.com/Editorial/Daily-News/AI-could-bring-9-increase-in-workers-on-assignment-Collaboration-in-Gig-Economy-gets-rolling-66878>